POOR MONEY HABIT:

Breaking Free from Financial Missteps

Audrey Karl

INTRODUCTION

UNDERSTANDING THE IMPACT OF POOR MONEY HABITS

Poor money habits can have far-reaching consequences that affect various aspects of our lives. These habits can create a cycle of financial stress and instability, impacting our present and future financial well-being. Here are some key points to consider when examining the impact of poor money habits:

1) Debt Accumulation: One of the most common consequences of poor money habits is the accumulation of debt. Overspending, relying on credit cards, and living beyond one's means can lead to high-interest debt that becomes difficult to manage. This debt not only affects your credit score but also limits your financial freedom and future opportunities.

2) Limited Savings: Poor money management often leads to inadequate savings. Without a proper savings strategy, you might struggle to cover unexpected expenses, emergencies, or future goals such as buying a house, funding education, or retiring comfortably. This lack of savings can perpetuate a cycle of financial instability.

3) Stress and Mental Health: Financial stress resulting from poor money habits can negatively impact mental health. Constantly worrying about bills, debt payments, and financial obligations can lead to anxiety, depression, and decreased overall well-being. This stress can also affect personal relationships and work performance.

4) Missed Investment Opportunities: Failing to invest wisely due to poor money habits can result in missed opportunities for wealth accumulation and financial growth. Delaying or neglecting investment planning can

hinder your ability to build wealth over time, potentially affecting your long-term financial security.

5) Inadequate Retirement Planning: Poor money habits can lead to inadequate retirement planning. Failing to contribute to retirement accounts and not prioritizing long-term financial goals can leave you ill-prepared for retirement, forcing you to work longer than desired or compromising your lifestyle in your later years.

6) Lack of Financial Literacy: Poor money habits often stem from a lack of financial literacy. Without understanding basic financial concepts such as budgeting, saving, investing, and managing credit, individuals are more likely to make poor financial decisions that impact their financial stability.

7) Impact on Relationships: Financial disagreements are a common source of conflict in relationships. Poor money habits can strain partnerships, marriages, and family relationships due to disagreements over spending, saving, and financial goals.

8) Opportunity Cost: Poor money habits also come with opportunity costs. Money spent on frivolous purchases or unnecessary expenses could have been used for more meaningful purposes, such as experiences, education, or investments that contribute to personal growth and financial stability.

9) Cyclical Nature: Poor money habits can create a cycle that's difficult to break. People who consistently make poor financial decisions might find themselves trapped in a pattern of debt and financial instability, making it challenging to improve their situation.

10) Long-Term Financial Goals: Poor money habits can significantly hinder the achievement of long-term financial goals. Whether it's buying a home, starting a business, or traveling, these goals require careful financial planning and discipline. Poor money habits can delay or even prevent the realization of such aspirations.

In conclusion, understanding the impact of poor money habits is crucial for maintaining financial well-being. By recognizing the consequences these habits can have on debt, savings, mental health, relationships, and long-term goals, individuals can take proactive steps to improve their financial habits. This includes educating themselves about financial literacy, creating a budget, managing debt responsibly, saving consistently, and seeking professional guidance when needed. By making positive changes to their money habits, individuals can pave the way for a more secure and fulfilling financial future.

THE PSYCHOLOGY OF MONEY HABITS

The psychology of money habits is a fascinating area of study that delves into the complex interplay between human behavior, financial decision-making, and long-term financial well-being. Our habits surrounding money are deeply rooted in psychological, emotional, and cognitive factors. Below are some considerable factors:

1) Behavioral Economics: The field of behavioral economics explores how psychological factors influence economic decisions. It highlights that humans often don't make rational decisions, but instead are influenced by cognitive biases, emotions, and social pressures. This has a significant impact on how we handle money.

2) Emotional Triggers: Money is not just a tool; it carries emotional weight. People often associate money with security, success, power, and even self-worth. These emotional associations can drive both positive and negative money habits. For example, emotional spending or retail therapy can be a result of seeking comfort or happiness through purchases.

3) Herd Mentality: People are highly influenced by the behavior of others, especially in financial matters. This can lead to herd mentality, where individuals make financial decisions based on the actions of those around them, rather than independent analysis. Herd behavior can result in bubbles in financial markets or unnecessary expenses.

4) Delayed Gratification: The ability to delay gratification is a key predictor of financial success. Individuals who can resist immediate rewards in favor of long-term goals tend to have healthier money habits. This trait is linked to self-control and the capacity to manage impulsive spending.

5) Anchoring and Framing: The way information is presented or framed can greatly impact financial decisions. Anchoring refers to the tendency to rely heavily on the first piece of information encountered when making decisions, while framing involves how options are presented. These cognitive biases can influence perceptions of value and impact spending choices.

6) Loss Aversion: The fear of loss is a powerful motivator. People often go to great lengths to avoid losses, even if it means making irrational decisions. This can lead to holding onto losing investments, refusing to cut losses, and avoiding risks that might be beneficial.

7) Money Personality Types: Different individuals have different money personalities. Some are savers, some are spenders, and others are risk-takers. Understanding your own money personality can help you make more aligned financial choices and develop healthier money habits.

8) Financial Childhood Experiences: Early experiences with money, including how it was discussed and managed in the family, can shape an individual's financial behavior in adulthood. For instance, growing up in an environment of scarcity or overspending can influence one's relationship with money.

9) Automated Decision-Making: Creating automated systems for saving, investing, and bill payments can mitigate the impact of impulsive decisions. By setting up these systems, individuals can take advantage of their cognitive biases, such as inertia, to foster positive money habits.

10) Behavioral Interventions: Researchers and experts have developed various strategies to help individuals improve their money habits. These interventions often involve setting specific goals, creating visual cues,

and implementing accountability mechanisms to encourage positive financial behavior.

In conclusion, the psychology of money habits is a multidimensional subject that encompasses cognitive biases, emotions, social influences, and past experiences. By understanding these factors, individuals can work toward cultivating healthier money habits and achieving greater financial well-being.

CHAPTER ONE

UNCOVERING THE ROOT CAUSES OF FINANCIAL MISSTEPS

Uncovering the root causes of financial missteps is essential for individuals, businesses, and even governments to understand and mitigate the risks associated with poor financial decision-making. Financial missteps can encompass a wide range of errors, including overspending, poor investment choices, debt accumulation, and failure to plan for the future. Identifying these root causes can help prevent such mistakes from happening and enable better financial management. Here are some key aspects to consider when delving into the root causes of financial missteps:

1) Lack of Financial Literacy: One of the primary reasons for financial missteps is a lack of understanding of basic financial concepts. Many individuals and even businesses struggle with financial literacy, which can lead to uninformed decisions, misunderstandings about interest rates, loans, and investments, and an overall inability to manage finances effectively.

2) Emotional Decision-Making: Emotions can heavily influence financial decisions. Fear, greed, and impulsiveness can lead to poor choices. Investors might panic during market downturns, leading them to sell off investments at a loss. Similarly, impulsive spending due to emotional triggers can result in accumulating debt.

3) Inadequate Planning: Failure to set clear financial goals and create a comprehensive budget can lead to overspending and inadequate savings. Without proper planning, individuals and businesses may not have a

clear roadmap for their financial future, making it difficult to make informed decisions.

4) Peer Pressure and Lifestyle Inflation: Keeping up with the spending habits of friends, family, or colleagues can lead to unnecessary expenditures. This phenomenon, known as lifestyle inflation, can cause individuals to overspend and neglect saving for future needs.

5) Risk Misperception: Misunderstanding or underestimating the risks associated with investments or financial decisions can result in significant losses. This can occur when individuals invest in complex financial products without fully comprehending the associated risks.

6) Overconfidence: Overestimating one's financial knowledge or investment skills can lead to risky decisions. Overconfident individuals may engage in speculative trading or make high-risk investments without proper research.

7) Ignoring Interest Rates: Failing to understand the impact of interest rates on loans and credit cards can result in accumulating high levels of debt. Ignoring the compounding effect of interest can lead to long-term financial challenges.

8) Inadequate Emergency Fund: Not having an emergency fund can make individuals vulnerable to unexpected expenses, leading to the use of credit cards or loans to cover these costs.

9) Herd Mentality: Following the crowd without conducting independent research can lead to financial missteps. This is particularly relevant in investment decisions, where herd mentality can cause assets to become overvalued or undervalued.

10) Complex Financial Products: Lack of understanding of complex financial instruments, such as derivatives or structured products, can result in significant losses. Investments in products with hidden risks can lead to unexpected financial downturns.

11) Inadequate Risk Management: Not having insurance coverage or underestimating potential risks, such as health issues or property damage, can lead to financial strain during emergencies.

12) Procrastination: Delaying financial decisions, such as retirement planning or debt repayment, can result in missed opportunities and increased financial stress over time.

In order to address these root causes and avoid financial missteps, individuals and entities should prioritize financial education, seek professional advice when needed, develop clear financial goals, establish a budget, practice disciplined decision-making, and continuously evaluate and adjust their financial strategies. Taking a proactive and informed approach to managing finances can significantly reduce the likelihood of falling victim to common financial pitfalls.

HOW BEHAVIORAL PATTERNS AFFECT YOUR FINANCES

Behavioral patterns have a profound impact on one's financial decisions and outcomes. These patterns encompass a wide range of psychological tendencies, biases, and habits that influence how individuals perceive, approach, and manage their finances. Understanding these patterns is crucial because they can either lead to financial success or contribute to detrimental outcomes.

1) Spending Habits: Behavioral patterns often determine how individuals spend their money. Impulse buying, emotional spending, and conspicuous consumption can lead to overspending, debt accumulation, and an inability to save effectively.

2) Delayed Gratification: The ability to delay immediate rewards for long-term financial gains is a key behavioral trait. Individuals who struggle with delayed gratification may struggle with saving, investing, and achieving financial goals.

3) Anchoring and Adjustment: People tend to rely heavily on initial pieces of information when making financial decisions. Anchoring to a certain price point or value can lead to unrealistic expectations or inappropriate judgments about the value of assets or investments.

4) Loss Aversion: The fear of loss often drives decisions more than the potential for gain. This can result in individuals holding onto losing investments for too long, missing out on opportunities, or avoiding calculated risks.

5) Confirmation Bias: People tend to seek information that confirms their existing beliefs and ignore contrary evidence. This can lead to poor investment choices if individuals only seek information that aligns with their preconceived notions.

6) Herd Mentality: Following the crowd without thorough analysis can lead to poor financial decisions. For instance, investing in a particular asset solely because others are doing so can lead to bubbles and crashes.

7) Overconfidence: Many individuals overestimate their financial knowledge and abilities. This can lead to excessive trading, overestimating investment returns, and making risky decisions.

8) Mental Accounting: People often categorize money into different mental accounts based on its source or intended use. This can lead to suboptimal decisions, such as treating a windfall differently from regular income.

9) Sunk Cost Fallacy: This refers to the tendency to continue investing in something based on the resources already committed, even if it no longer makes financial sense. It can lead to holding onto failing investments or projects.

10) Behavioral Biases: Numerous cognitive biases, such as availability bias, framing effects, and endowment effect, influence financial choices. These biases can result in suboptimal asset allocation, investment decisions, and risk management.

11) Financial Goal Setting: Behavioral patterns play a role in how individuals set and pursue financial goals. Setting realistic, achievable goals and breaking them down into smaller steps can help overcome procrastination and improve financial outcomes.

12) Budgeting and Saving: Effective budgeting requires discipline and self-control, which are influenced by behavioral patterns. The ability to allocate funds for different purposes and stick to a budget can impact long-term financial stability.

Recognizing these behavioral patterns and actively working to mitigate their negative effects is essential for financial success. Techniques such as mindfulness, financial education, seeking advice, and setting up systems that counteract these biases can help individuals make more rational and informed financial decisions.

IDENTIFYING YOUR POOR MONEY HABITS

Identifying your poor money habits is a crucial step towards achieving financial stability and success. These habits can significantly impact your financial well-being over time, often leading to debt, limited savings, and stress. Here's an extensive guide on how to identify and address your poor money habits:

1) Self-Awareness: Start by recognizing that you may have poor money habits. This requires an honest assessment of your financial behaviors, decisions, and patterns.

2) Track Your Spending: Keep a detailed record of every expense for a month or two. Categorize your spending to identify where your money is going. This will reveal areas where you might be overspending or making unnecessary purchases.

3) Review Your Bank Statements: Regularly review your bank and credit card statements to identify recurring expenses and irregular spending. This can help you uncover subscriptions or services you no longer use.

4) Identify Emotional Triggers: Often, poor money habits are tied to emotions such as stress, boredom, or happiness. Recognize situations that trigger impulsive spending or excessive splurging.

5) Assess Impulse Purchases: Take note of items you bought on a whim and rarely use. This indicates impulsive spending habits that can drain your finances.

6) Evaluate Debt Levels: High levels of credit card debt, personal loans, or unpaid bills are clear signs of poor money management. These debts can accumulate quickly if not managed properly.

7) Analyze Savings Patterns: Review your savings history. Are you consistently saving a portion of your income, or do you struggle to save at all? Inadequate savings can indicate poor money habits.

8) Consider Financial Goals: If you lack clear financial goals or a plan to achieve them, it's a sign of poor money habits. Without goals, you might not have the motivation to make wise financial decisions.

9) Review Investment Choices: If you're investing without proper research or making impulsive investment decisions, you might be falling victim to poor investment habits.

10) Communication About Finances: Discuss money matters with family members or a partner. Poor communication about finances can lead to misunderstandings and poor financial decisions.

11) Avoiding Budgeting: Neglecting to create and stick to a budget can lead to overspending and not knowing where your money is going.

12) Neglecting Financial Education: If you're not actively seeking knowledge about personal finance, you might be missing out on opportunities to improve your financial habits.

13) Living Beyond Your Means: Continuously spending more than you earn can lead to debt and financial stress. Recognize signs of living beyond your means, such as relying on credit cards to cover basic expenses.

14) Failing to Plan for the Future: Ignoring retirement planning, emergency funds, and insurance needs can leave you financially vulnerable in the long run.

15) Reviewing Long-Term Trends: Look at your financial behavior over several months or years. Are you consistently making the same poor money decisions?

Once you've identified your poor money habits, it's time to take action:

1) Set Clear Goals: Define short-term and long-term financial goals to provide direction and motivation for improving your habits.

2) Create a Budget: Develop a realistic budget that allocates funds to necessities, savings, and discretionary spending.

3) Educate Yourself: Learn about personal finance, budgeting, investing, and debt management to make informed decisions.

4) Practice Self-Control: Before making a purchase, give yourself time to consider whether it aligns with your goals and needs, rather than giving in to impulses.

5) Limit Temptations: Unsubscribe from shopping emails, avoid window shopping, and limit exposure to situations that trigger impulsive spending.

6) Savings: Set up automatic transfers to your savings and investment accounts to ensure consistent contributions.

7) Review Regularly: Continuously monitor your progress, adjust your budget as needed, and celebrate achievements.

8) Seek Professional Help: If your poor money habits are deeply ingrained or leading to significant financial distress, consider seeking help from a financial advisor or counselor.

Remember, changing habits takes time and effort. Be patient with yourself as you work towards improving your relationship with money.

CHAPTER TWO

SELF-REFLECTION AND AWARENESS

Self-reflection and awareness are fundamental aspects of personal growth and development. They involve the ability to introspectively examine one's thoughts, emotions, behaviors, and experiences, leading to a deeper understanding of oneself. This process is a cornerstone of emotional intelligence and can have profound effects on various aspects of life, including relationships, decision-making, and overall well-being.

Self-reflection involves taking the time to contemplate and analyze one's thoughts, actions, and experiences. It requires a certain level of mindfulness and willingness to confront both positive and negative aspects of oneself. Through self-reflection, individuals can identify patterns of behavior, triggers for emotional responses, and underlying beliefs that shape their perceptions of the world.

Awareness, on the other hand, encompasses the ability to be present in the moment and fully attuned to one's surroundings, emotions, and thoughts. It involves cultivating a state of mindfulness that allows individuals to observe their internal experiences without judgment. This heightened awareness enables individuals to respond to situations rather than react impulsively, fostering better control over their behavior and emotions.

Both self-reflection and awareness are interconnected processes that feed into each other. Self-reflection leads to increased self-awareness, as individuals begin to recognize their strengths, weaknesses, values, and aspirations. On the other hand, heightened awareness facilitates more effective self-reflection, as individuals become attuned to their inner experiences and are better equipped to analyze and understand them.

Practicing self-reflection and awareness often involves various techniques, such as journaling, meditation, mindfulness exercises, and seeking feedback from trusted individuals. Keeping a reflective journal allows individuals to document their thoughts and experiences over time, aiding in the identification of patterns and changes in behavior. Meditation and mindfulness practices train the mind to focus on the present moment, enhancing awareness of one's thoughts and emotions as they arise.

Benefits of cultivating self-reflection and awareness are multifaceted. They enable individuals to:

1) Enhance Emotional Intelligence: By understanding their emotions and the underlying reasons behind them, individuals can develop better emotional regulation and empathy towards others.

2) Improve Decision-Making: Self-awareness helps individuals recognize their values and priorities, leading to more aligned and thoughtful decision-making.

3) Strengthen Relationships: Understanding one's triggers and communication patterns can lead to healthier interactions and improved relationships.

4) Personal Growth: Identifying areas for improvement and setting meaningful goals becomes easier when one is attuned to their strengths and weaknesses.

5) Reduce Stress: Being present and aware of one's thoughts can reduce rumination about the past or anxiety about the future, leading to decreased stress levels.

6) Enhance Creativity: Increased self-awareness can uncover hidden talents and perspectives, fostering creativity and innovation.

7) Boost Resilience: Self-reflection allows individuals to understand how they have overcome challenges in the past, increasing their ability to cope with future difficulties.

8) Authenticity: When individuals know themselves deeply, they can live more authentically by aligning their actions with their true selves.

It's Important to note that self-reflection and awareness are ongoing processes that require patience and commitment. They involve confronting uncomfortable truths, acknowledging vulnerabilities, and being open to change. Engaging in these practices can be challenging, but the rewards in terms of personal growth and well-being are significant. As individuals continue to delve into their inner selves, they can foster a greater sense of purpose, fulfillment, and a deeper connection with the world around them.

COMMON FINANCIAL PITFALLS TO WATCH OUT FOR

Certainly! Avoiding financial pitfalls is crucial for maintaining a healthy financial situation. Below are some financial pitfall that should be avoided:

1) Living Beyond Your Means: Spending more than you earn can quickly lead to debt. It's important to create a budget, track your expenses, and prioritize needs over wants.

2) Not Having an Emergency Fund: Without an emergency fund, unexpected expenses can lead to financial stress or even debt. Aim to have 3-6 months' worth of living expenses set aside in a savings account.

3) High-Interest Debt: Accumulating high-interest debt, such as credit card debt, can be financially draining. Strive to pay off high-interest debts as quickly as possible to avoid excessive interest payments.

4) Neglecting Retirement Savings: Not saving for retirement early enough can lead to a shortfall in your golden years. Start saving for retirement as soon as possible and take advantage of employer-sponsored plans like 401(k)s.

5) Overlooking Insurance Needs: Not having adequate insurance coverage, such as health, auto, home, or life insurance, can leave you vulnerable to significant financial setbacks in the event of accidents, illnesses, or disasters.

6) Failing to Invest Wisely: Not investing or making impulsive investment decisions can hinder wealth-building opportunities. Educate yourself about different investment options and consider seeking professional advice.

7) Ignoring Financial Goals: Lack of clear financial goals can lead to aimless spending and poor money management. Set short-term and long-term financial goals to stay focused on your priorities.

8) Not Reviewing Financial Statements: Neglecting to review bank statements, credit card bills, and other financial statements can lead to missed errors, fraudulent activities, or oversights.

9) Impulse Buying: Giving in to impulsive purchases without considering their impact on your budget can quickly add up and strain your finances.

10) Not Negotiating: Whether it's your salary, bills, or contracts, failing to negotiate can lead to missed opportunities for saving or earning more money.

11) Co-signing Loans: Co-signing a loan for someone else can put your credit and finances at risk if the borrower defaults. Be cautious before co-signing and understand the potential consequences.

12) Ignoring Interest Rates: Ignoring fluctuating interest rates on loans or mortgages can result in missed chances to refinance and save money over the long term.

13) Relying Solely on Credit: Depending solely on credit cards for purchases can lead to overspending and accumulating debt.

14) Not Diversifying Investments: Putting all your investments in one asset or industry can expose you to higher risks. Diversify your investment portfolio to mitigate potential losses.

15) Underestimating Small Expenses: Small, recurring expenses can add up over time. Keep track of subscriptions, memberships, and other recurring costs to avoid overspending.

Avoiding these financial pitfalls requires awareness, discipline, and proactive decision-making. Regularly reviewing your financial situation and seeking guidance from financial professionals can help you stay on track towards achieving your financial goals.

THE PATH TO FINANCIAL FREEDOM

The Path to Financial Freedom is a journey that involves careful planning, disciplined habits, and a solid understanding of personal finance. It's the process of attaining a level of financial stability where you have the means to support your desired lifestyle without constantly worrying about money. This journey can be broken down into several key components:

1) Financial Education: The first step is to educate yourself about basic financial concepts. This includes understanding budgeting, saving, investing, debt management, and various investment vehicles. Taking the time to learn about these topics will empower you to make informed decisions about your money.

2) Setting Clear Goals: Financial freedom is different for everyone. It might involve paying off debts, saving for a comfortable retirement, buying a home, or funding a passion project. Setting clear and achievable financial goals is crucial, as these goals will guide your decisions and keep you motivated.

3) Creating a Budget: A budget is the foundation of financial planning. Creating a budget allows you to allocate your money efficiently, cut unnecessary spending, and ensure you're living within your means.

4) Saving and Investing: Saving a portion of your income is essential for building an emergency fund and meeting short-term goals. However, achieving financial freedom often requires investing to grow your wealth over time. Diversified investments, such as stocks, bonds, real estate, and mutual funds, can help your money work for you.

5) Debt Management: Paying off high-interest debt should be a priority. High-interest debts can accumulate quickly and hinder your progress toward financial freedom. Once you've cleared high-interest debts, you can focus on managing and leveraging low-interest debts, like a mortgage.

6) Living Below Your Means: Consistently spending less than you earn is a key principle of financial freedom. It allows you to save and invest more, which accelerates your journey towards your financial goals.

7) Passive Income Streams: Building passive income streams, such as rental income, dividends, or royalties, can provide a consistent cash flow without requiring constant effort. Passive income can significantly contribute to your financial stability and freedom.

8) Continued Learning and Adaptation: The world of finance is dynamic. Staying updated with financial trends, economic shifts, and new investment opportunities is crucial.

9) Patience and Discipline: Achieving financial freedom is a marathon, not a sprint. It requires patience and discipline to stay on track, especially during challenging times or periods of market volatility.

10) Estate Planning: As you accumulate wealth, it's important to plan for the future by creating a will, setting up trusts, and making arrangements for the orderly transfer of your assets. Estate planning ensures that your financial legacy is managed according to your wishes.

Remember that the path to financial freedom is not a linear process. It involves making adjustments, learning from mistakes, and staying committed to your goals. Every individual's journey is unique, influenced by personal circumstances, risk tolerance, and aspirations.The key is to start early, stay consistent, and keep your long-term vision in mind.

CHAPTER THREE

SETTING CLEAR FINANCIAL GOALS

Setting clear financial goals is a crucial step towards achieving financial success and securing your future. Without well-defined goals, it's easy to drift aimlessly through life, making impulsive decisions that might not align with your long-term aspirations. Whether your goals involve buying a home, saving for retirement, paying off debt, or going on a dream vacation, having a structured plan in place can make a significant difference.

1) Define Your Goals: Start by identifying your financial aspirations. These could be short-term goals like paying off credit card debt, medium-term goals like saving for a down payment on a house, or long-term goals like building a retirement fund.

2) Quantify Your Goals: Assign a monetary value to each goal. This provides clarity and allows you to determine how much you need to save or invest to reach your target. For instance, if you're planning to buy a house, calculate the down payment and associated costs.

3) Prioritize: Not all goals are equally important. It might be helpful to categorize goals as essential (e.g., building an emergency fund), important (e.g., saving for a child's education), and aspirational (e.g., luxury travel).

4) Break Down Goals: Divide big goals into smaller, manageable steps. This makes the process less daunting and helps you track your progress.

For instance, if you're aiming to save $50,000 for a down payment, break it into monthly or yearly saving targets.

5) Establish Timeframes: Allocate deadlines to your objectives. The presence of a designated timeframe instills a feeling of immediacy, deterring procrastination. Additionally, it aids in strategic planning and optimal resource distribution.

6) Consider Financial Constraints: Evaluate your current financial situation and identify potential constraints. This might involve analyzing your income, expenses, and debt. Realistic goal-setting considers your financial limitations while still pushing you to achieve more.

7) Research and Plan: Research the steps required to achieve your goals. If you're investing, learn about different investment options. If you're saving for education, understand the costs and potential funding sources.

8) Monitor and Adjust: Regularly review your progress. If you're falling behind, reassess your strategy. Life circumstances can change, and your goals might need adjustment. Be flexible while staying focused on the end result.

9) Celebrate Milestones: Recognize and celebrate your achievements along the way. This boosts motivation and makes the journey towards your larger goal more enjoyable.

10) Seek Professional Advice: Depending on your goals, it might be beneficial to consult financial advisors, tax professionals, or investment experts.

11) Accountability: Share your goals with a trusted friend or family member who can hold you accountable. This external encouragement can help you stay on track, especially during challenging times.

12) Visualize Your Success: Imagine how your life will improve once you achieve your financial goals. Visualization can inspire you to remain disciplined and dedicated to your plan.

In conclusion, setting clear financial goals is a cornerstone of effective financial management. It provides direction, purpose, and a roadmap for your financial journey. By following these steps and staying committed, you can work towards achieving your aspirations and securing your financial future.

BUILDING A STRONG FOUNDATION FOR BETTER HABITS

Building a strong foundation for better habits is essential for personal growth and positive transformation. Habits play a crucial role in shaping our behaviors and ultimately determining our success and well-being. Here's an extensive guide on how to establish a solid foundation for cultivating better habits:

1) Self-awareness: Begin by identifying the habits you currently have and understanding their impact on your life. Reflect on both positive and negative habits, as well as the triggers that lead to them. This self-awareness forms the basis for change.

2) Clear Goals: Define what you want to achieve through new habits. Whether it's improved health, increased productivity, or enhanced relationships, having clear goals provides direction and motivation.

3) Start Small: Begin with one or two habits that are manageable and achievable. Starting small prevents overwhelm and increases the likelihood of success.

4) Consistency: Consistency is key to habit formation. Commit to performing the desired behavior daily or at a set frequency. Consistency reinforces the neural pathways associated with the habit, making it more automatic over time.

5) Create Triggers: Associate your new habit with an existing cue or trigger. For example, if you want to develop a habit of stretching in the

morning, do it right after brushing your teeth. This linkage makes the habit easier to remember and execute.

6) Accountability: Share your goals with a friend, family member, or mentor who can hold you accountable. Reporting your progress to someone else increases your commitment to sticking with the habit.

7) Creating a Supportive Setting: Establish a positive environment that encourages your desired habits. For instance, if you're aiming to improve your eating habits, fill your kitchen with nourishing foods and eliminate unhealthy snacks.

8) Use Rewards: Reward yourself for successfully practicing the habit. Positive reinforcement strengthens the habit loop in your brain. However, ensure the rewards align with your overall goal – for example, don't reward yourself with junk food if you're trying to eat better.

9) Mindfulness and Reflection: Practice mindfulness to become more aware of your actions and thoughts. Regularly reflect on your progress, challenges, and adjustments needed. This self-reflection helps you stay on track and adapt your approach as necessary.

10) Overcoming Setbacks: Setbacks are natural when building habits. Instead of getting discouraged, view them as learning opportunities. Analyze what led to the setback and strategize how to prevent it in the future.

11) Tracking and Measurement: Keep a record of your habit-related activities. Use a journal, app, or calendar to track your progress. Monitoring your consistency and incremental improvements can be motivating.

12) Education and Skill-Building: Equip yourself with the knowledge and skills needed for the habit. If you're trying to incorporate regular exercise, for instance, learn about proper techniques and safe practices.

13) Flexibility: Be willing to adjust your approach if a habit isn't working as planned. Flexibility doesn't mean giving up; it means finding alternative methods that suit your personality and circumstances better.

14) Patience: Habits take time to develop. Research suggests that it takes around 66 days on average for a behavior to become a habit. Be patient and persistent in your efforts.

15) Celebrate Progress: Acknowledge and celebrate your achievements along the way. Small victories contribute to your overall sense of accomplishment and motivate you to continue building better habits.

Remember, building a strong foundation for better habits is a continuous journey. The process requires dedication, self-compassion, and a willingness to learn and adapt. Over time, the habits you cultivate will become an integral part of your lifestyle, contributing to your personal and professional growth.

BREAKING BAD HABITS

Breaking bad habits can be a challenging yet immensely rewarding endeavor. Habits are deeply ingrained patterns of behavior that we often engage in without conscious thought. Whether it's biting your nails, overeating, procrastinating, or smoking, bad habits can have detrimental effects on our physical, mental, and emotional well-being. Here's a comprehensive guide on how to effectively break free from these patterns:

1) Self-Awareness: The first step is recognizing the habit you want to change. Be honest with yourself about why you engage in it, the triggers that prompt it, and the consequences it brings.

2) Set Clear Intentions: Clearly define your reasons for wanting to break the habit. Whether it's improving your health, boosting productivity, or

enhancing your relationships, having a strong motivation will fuel your determination.

3) Small: Trying to completely eliminate a habit overnight can be overwhelming. Begin with small, manageable changes. For instance, if you're trying to cut down on sugar intake, start by reducing the amount of sugar in your coffee.

4) Replace with Positive Behavior: Habits often fill a void or meet a need. Replace the negative habit with a positive behavior that fulfills the same need. If you're trying to quit mindless snacking, replace it with a healthier snack or a short walk.

5) Identify Triggers: Pinpoint the situations, emotions, or environments that trigger the habit. This awareness allows you to develop strategies to avoid or cope with these triggers effectively.

6) Create a Support System: Share your goal with friends, family, or a support group. Having people who encourage and hold you accountable can significantly increase your chances of success.

7) Use Positive Reinforcement: Reward yourself for each milestone achieved. This could be treating yourself to something enjoyable, as it helps associate breaking the habit with positive outcomes.

8) Practice Mindfulness: Mindfulness techniques can help you become more conscious of your actions and impulses. This awareness enables you to pause and make a conscious choice instead of falling into automatic behaviors.

9) Visualize Success: Visualize yourself successfully breaking the habit. This mental imagery enhances your belief in your ability to change and reinforces your commitment.

10) Learn from Relapses: It's common to experience setbacks along the way. Instead of viewing relapses as failures, treat them as learning opportunities. Analyze what triggered the relapse and develop strategies to handle similar situations better in the future.

11) Persistence is Key: Breaking a habit takes time and effort. Stay patient and persistent. Remember that change is a process, and setbacks don't define your journey.

12) Seek Professional Help: For deeply ingrained or addictive habits, seeking help from a therapist, counselor, or support group can provide valuable guidance and strategies.

13) Modify Your Environment: Make changes in your surroundings to reduce the temptation to engage in the habit. For instance, if you're trying to reduce screen time, keep devices out of sight during designated periods.

14) Track Your Progress: Keep a journal or use habit-tracking apps to monitor your progress. This helps you stay accountable and see how far you've come.

15) Celebrate Milestones: Celebrate your achievements at various stages. Breaking a habit is a significant accomplishment, and acknowledging your progress boosts your self-confidence.

Remember that breaking bad habits is a journey that requires commitment, self-compassion, and resilience. It's about making consistent choices that align with your desired outcomes. With time, effort, and the right strategies, you can successfully overcome even the most entrenched habits.

CHAPTER FOUR

STRATEGIES FOR OVERCOMING IMPULSE SPENDING

Impulse spending, also known as impulsive buying or emotional buying, refers to the act of making unplanned purchases on a whim without considering the long-term consequences. This behavior can have a negative impact on personal finances and overall financial well-being. To overcome impulse spending, consider implementing the following strategies:

1) Create a Budget: Establish a clear and realistic budget that outlines your monthly income, expenses, and savings goals. Knowing exactly how much you can spend on discretionary items can help you make informed decisions and curb impulse buying.

2) Identify Triggers: Recognize the situations, emotions, or environments that trigger your impulse spending. Whether it's stress, boredom, peer pressure, or retail displays, understanding your triggers can help you avoid or manage them effectively.

3) Practice Mindful Shopping: Before making a purchase, take a moment to pause and ask yourself whether you truly need the item. Consider whether it aligns with your budget, values, and long-term goals. Mindful shopping encourages intentional decision-making.

4) Implement a Waiting Period: Implement a waiting period before making non-essential purchases. For example, give yourself 24 hours or a week to reconsider the purchase. This delay can help you evaluate whether the item is a genuine need or just a passing desire.

5) Use Shopping Lists: Prepare a detailed shopping list before heading to the store or shopping online. Stick to the list and avoid deviating from it, even if you come across tempting deals or items.

6) Avoid Impulse Environments: Limit exposure to environments that encourage impulsive spending, such as malls or online shopping platforms. Unsubscribe from promotional emails and unfollow social media accounts that frequently showcase products.

7) Set Financial Goals: Establish short-term and long-term financial goals, such as saving for a vacation, buying a home, or paying off debt. Focusing on these goals can motivate you to prioritize saving over impulsive purchases.

8) Use Cash or Debit Cards: Leave credit cards at home when you go shopping, and opt for cash or a debit card instead. Physical payment methods make the spending process more tangible, helping you become more conscious of your purchases.

9) Practice Self-Care: Find healthy and constructive ways to manage emotions like stress, anxiety, or boredom. Engage in activities you enjoy, exercise, meditate, or spend time with loved ones to reduce the urge to shop impulsively.

10) Unsubscribe and Unfollow: Clear your inbox of retail emails and unfollow brands on social media that consistently tempt you with offers and promotions. Less exposure to such marketing can reduce the temptation to spend impulsively.

11) Compare Prices: Before purchasing, take time to research and compare prices across different stores or online platforms. This not only helps you find the best deal but also gives you time to reconsider the purchase.

12) Track Your Spending: Keep a record of all your expenses, including small purchases. Reviewing your spending patterns can highlight areas where impulse spending is occurring and help you make necessary adjustments.

Remember that overcoming impulse spending is a gradual process that requires self-awareness and discipline. Implementing these strategies consistently can help you regain control over your spending habits and work toward a more financially secure future.

MANAGING PROCRASTINATION AND AVOIDANCE

Managing procrastination and avoidance is crucial for maintaining productivity and achieving one's goals. Procrastination refers to the act of delaying tasks that need to be completed, often opting for short-term pleasure or comfort instead. Avoidance, on the other hand, involves intentionally evading tasks that may trigger discomfort, anxiety, or stress. Both tendencies can hinder personal and professional growth, but there are several strategies to effectively manage them:

1) Self-Awareness: Recognizing when you're procrastinating or avoiding tasks is the first step. Reflect on your behaviors and thoughts to identify patterns and triggers. This awareness will help you intervene early and implement strategies to overcome these tendencies.

2) Break Tasks into Smaller Steps: Large tasks can feel overwhelming and lead to avoidance. Break them into smaller, manageable steps. Completing these smaller portions can provide a sense of accomplishment and motivate you to continue working.

3) Set Clear Goals: Define specific, measurable, achievable, relevant, and time-bound (SMART) goals. Clarity about what needs to be achieved and by when can reduce the tendency to procrastinate.

4) Use Time Management Techniques: Techniques like the Pomodoro Technique (working for a focused 25-minute period followed by a 5-minute break) can enhance concentration and reduce the likelihood of procrastination.

5) Prioritize Tasks: Arrange tasks in order of importance. Tackling high-priority tasks first can reduce the inclination to procrastinate on less important tasks.

6) Create a Routine: Establishing a daily routine can help eliminate decision fatigue and create a structured environment that minimizes opportunities for avoidance.

7) Minimize Distractions: Identify and minimize sources of distraction, such as social media, emails, or noisy environments. This can help you maintain focus on the task at hand.

8) Reward Mechanism: Establish a system of incentives for timely task completion. Grant yourself a pleasant indulgence upon accomplishing each task, thereby reinforcing constructive behavior.

9) Mindfulness and Self-Compassion: Practicing mindfulness can help you become more aware of your thoughts and emotions, reducing the likelihood of avoidance. Self-compassion can counteract negative self-talk and promote a more forgiving attitude toward setbacks.

10) Visualize Success and Consequences: Imagine the positive outcomes of completing a task and the negative consequences of avoiding it. This mental exercise can motivate you to take action.

11) Accountability: Share your goals with a friend, family member, or colleague who can hold you accountable. Knowing that someone is tracking your progress can discourage procrastination.

12) Manage Perfectionism: Perfectionism can lead to avoidance due to fear of failure. Shift your focus from perfection to progress and learning. Embrace mistakes and work on them.

13) Limit Planning: While planning is essential, excessive planning can become a form of procrastination itself. Set a time limit for planning and commit to taking action afterward.

14) Understand Resistance: Explore the reasons behind your resistance to certain tasks. Identifying underlying fears or negative beliefs can help you address them directly.

15) Seek Professional Help: If procrastination or avoidance significantly impairs your daily life or mental well-being, consider seeking support from a therapist or counselor who specializes in cognitive-behavioral techniques.

Implementing these strategies and adapting them to your personal preferences can help you become more productive, achieve your goals, and lead a more fulfilling life.

CULTIVATING HEALTHY MONEY HABITS

Cultivating healthy money habits is essential for achieving financial stability and long-term success. These habits are the building blocks of sound financial management and can have a profound impact on your overall well-being. Below are few practices to consider:

1) Budgeting: Begin by crafting a budget that details your monthly earnings and expenditures. This will enable you to monitor your spending patterns, pinpoint opportunities for reduction or savings.

2) Expense Tracking: Maintain a log of all expenditures, regardless of their size. This practice will provide you with a transparent overview of your spending trends, aiding you in making well-informed choices regarding fund allocation.

3) Living Within Your Means: Avoid overspending and try to live within your means. This means not relying heavily on credit cards or loans to finance your lifestyle.

4) Emergency Fund: Build an emergency fund that covers three to six months' worth of living expenses. This will provide a safety net in case of unexpected events like medical emergencies or job loss.

5) Consistent Savings: Cultivate the practice of setting aside a portion of your earnings on a routine basis. Streamline the process by arranging automated transfers to a dedicated savings account.

6) Setting Financial Goals: Define both short-term and long-term financial goals. These could include paying off debt, buying a home, saving for retirement, or taking a dream vacation.

7) Debt Management: Prioritize paying off high-interest debts like credit card balances. Create a plan to tackle your debts systematically while still maintaining your other financial obligations.

8) Wisely: Educate yourself about different investment options and consider seeking professional advice. Investing can help your money grow over time and work towards your long-term goals.

9) Delayed Gratification: Practice delayed gratification by distinguishing between needs and wants. Before making a purchase, give yourself time to think if it aligns with your financial goals.

10) Avoid Impulse Buying: Impulse purchases can derail your budget. Make a habit of waiting a day or two before making non-essential purchases to ensure you genuinely need or want the item.

11) Regular Review: Periodically review your financial situation, including your budget, savings, investments, and debts.

12) Continuous Learning: Stay informed about personal finance topics. Read books, articles, and attend workshops to enhance your financial literacy and decision-making skills.

13) Avoid Comparison: Everyone's financial journey is different. Avoid comparing your progress to others, as this can lead to unnecessary stress and poor financial decisions.

14) Negotiate and Shop Smart: Negotiate for better deals, and shop around for discounts or better prices before making significant purchases.

15) Mindful Spending: Practice mindful spending by considering the value a purchase adds to your life. Focus on experiences and items that genuinely contribute to your well-being and happiness.

16) Regularly Review Financial Goals: Revisit your financial goals and adjust them as needed based on changes in your life circumstances, income, and priorities.

Remember, cultivating healthy money habits is a gradual process that requires discipline and consistency. By implementing these practices, you can create a strong foundation for financial success and reduce stress related to money management.

CHAPTER FIVE

BUDGETING AND TRACKING YOUR EXPENSE

Budgeting and tracking expenses are essential financial practices that help individuals and households manage their money effectively. These practices provide a clear overview of income, spending habits, and financial goals, enabling better decision-making and ensuring financial stability. Let's delve into the details of budgeting and expense tracking:

Budgeting:
Budgeting involves creating a plan for how you will allocate your income across various categories such as housing, transportation, groceries, entertainment, savings, and more. The primary goal of budgeting is to ensure that your expenses do not exceed your income, allowing you to achieve your financial objectives. Tips on how to create an effective budget includes:

1) Calculate Income: Start by determining your total monthly income, including salaries, bonuses, side gigs, and any other sources of revenue.

2) Identify Fixed Expenses: List your fixed expenses, such as rent/mortgage, utilities, insurance, and loan payments. These are consistent amounts that need to be paid regularly.

3) List Variable Expenses: Identify variable expenses like groceries, dining out, entertainment, and discretionary spending. These expenses may not be the same from months to months.

4) Set Financial Goals: Define short-term and long-term financial goals, such as building an emergency fund, saving for a vacation, or paying off debt. Allocate funds towards these goals in your budget.

5) Allocate Categories: Divide your income into categories based on your expenses. Assign limits to each category, ensuring that your total expenses are lower than your income.

6) Track Progress: Regularly review your budget to track your progress. Adjust your allocations as needed to stay on track and accommodate changes in your financial situation.

Expense Tracking:
Expense tracking involves monitoring and recording every expense you make. This practice helps you understand your spending patterns, identify areas where you can cut back, and stay accountable to your budget. Here's how to effectively track your expenses:

1) Choose Tracking Method: Decide whether you want to track expenses manually using a notebook or spreadsheet or use digital tools and apps for automated tracking.

2) Categorize Expenses: Categorize your expenses into groups like groceries, utilities, transportation, entertainment, and more. This will help you analyze your spending patterns.

3) Every Expense: Consistently record every expense, no matter how small. This includes cash purchases, credit/debit card transactions, and online payments.

4) Review Regularly: Set a specific time each week or month to review your tracked expenses. Compare your spending against your budget to see if you're staying on track.

5) Analyze Trends: Look for patterns and trends in your spending. Are there categories where you consistently overspend? Identifying these areas will help you make adjustments.

6) Adjust Your Budget: Based on the insights gained from expense tracking, adjust your budget as necessary. You might need to reallocate funds or make conscious efforts to reduce spending in certain areas.

7) Stay Disciplined: Expense tracking requires discipline and consistency. Stay committed to recording every expense to get an accurate picture of your financial situation.

In summary, budgeting and tracking expenses are powerful tools that promote financial awareness and discipline. By creating a well-structured budget and diligently tracking your spending, you can work towards achieving your financial goals, minimizing debt, and building a more secure financial future.

SAVING AND INVESTING WISELY

Certainly! Saving and investing wisely are crucial components of financial planning that can help individuals achieve their long-term financial goals, build wealth, and secure their future. Let's delve into each of these aspects in detail.

Saving Wisely:

Saving involves setting aside a portion of your income for future needs and unexpected expenses. Here are some key principles for saving wisely:

1) Set Clear Goals: Determine your financial objectives, such as creating an emergency fund, saving for a home, education, retirement, or other specific goals.

2) Budgeting: Budgeting involves crafting a financial plan to monitor your earnings and expenditures. This aids in pinpointing areas where reductions can be made, allowing for greater contributions to savings.

3) Establish a Fund: Construct an emergency fund capable of covering living expenses for 3 to 6 months. This fund serves as a safety cushion for unforeseen situations such as medical crises or unemployment.

4) Automate Savings: Set up automatic transfers to a separate savings account. This ensures a consistent saving habit and prevents you from spending money before saving.

5) Debt Management: Prioritize paying off high-interest debts to save on interest payments. This frees up more money that can be directed towards savings.

Investing Wisely:

Investing involves putting your money into assets with the potential to grow over time. Here are important considerations for investing wisely:

1) Comprehend Risk and Reward: Every investment bears a degree of risk. Increased potential profits are frequently linked with heightened risk. Evaluate your risk tolerance and make investments in alignment with it.

2) Diversification: Disperse your investments among various asset categories (such as stocks, bonds, real estate, etc.) to minimize risk. Diversification aids in lessening losses in case a particular investment performs poorly.

3) Time Horizon: Consider your investment timeline. Short-term goals may warrant more conservative investments, while long-term goals can tolerate more risk for potentially higher returns.

4) Research and Education: Thoroughly research investments before committing funds. Understand the market trends, historical performance, and the company's financial health if you're investing in stocks.

5) Costs and Fees: Be aware of investment fees, such as management fees for mutual funds or transaction fees for buying/selling stocks.

6) Avoid Emotional Decision-Making: Market fluctuations are natural. Avoid making impulsive decisions based on short-term market movements. Stick to your long-term investment strategy.

7) Regular Review: Periodically review your investment portfolio to ensure it aligns with your goals and risk tolerance. Rebalancing may be necessary to maintain your desired asset allocation.

8) Professional Advice: Consider seeking advice from financial advisors or investment professionals. They can provide personalized guidance based on your financial situation and goals.

Remember that saving and investing wisely are ongoing processes. Adjustments may be needed as your life circumstances change.Both saving and investing require discipline, patience, and a long-term perspective to reap the benefits of compounding growth over time.

NAVIGATING CREDIT AND DEBT

Navigating credit and debt is a crucial aspect of personal finance management. It involves understanding how credit works, using it wisely, and managing debt responsibly to maintain financial health and avoid potential pitfalls. Take a deep dive into the subject with this comprehensive analysis:

Understanding Credit:
Credit refers to the ability to borrow money with the promise of repayment in the future. It enables individuals to make purchases, invest, or handle emergencies without having to pay upfront. Credit is typically extended in various forms, including credit cards, loans, and lines of credit. To navigate credit effectively, it's important to understand key concepts:

1) Credit Score: Your credit score, often represented as a three-digit number, reflects your creditworthiness. It's based on factors such as payment history, credit utilization, length of credit history, types of credit, and recent credit inquiries.

2) Credit Report: This is a detailed record of your credit history, including accounts, payment history, and any negative items. Regularly reviewing your credit report helps you identify errors and maintain accurate information.

3) Credit Utilization: This is the ratio of your credit card balances to your credit limits. Keeping this ratio low (typically below 30%) demonstrates responsible credit use and can positively impact your credit score.

Using Credit Wisely:
To navigate credit successfully, consider the following tips:

1) Craft a Budget: Formulate a budget to monitor your earnings and expenditures. This enables you to earmark funds for credit payments and averts excessive spending.

2) Pay On Time: Timely payments are crucial for maintaining a good credit score. Late payments can lead to increased interest rates and negative impacts on your credit history.

3) Avoid Overspending: Just because you have available credit doesn't mean you should use it all. Only borrow what you can comfortably repay to avoid accumulating unnecessary debt.

4) Diversify Credit: Having a mix of credit types (e.g., credit cards, installment loans) can positively affect your credit score, as it shows your ability to manage different types of credit.

Managing Debt:
Debt management involves handling existing debts effectively to avoid financial strain and ensure long-term financial well-being:

1) Prioritize High-Interest Debt: Pay off high-interest debts, such as credit card balances, first. The interest on these debts can accumulate quickly and hinder your ability to pay down the principal.

2) Debt Snowball vs. Debt Avalanche: Two popular debt repayment strategies are the snowball method (paying off smallest debts first) and the avalanche method (paying off highest-interest debts first). Choose the approach that suits your financial situation and psychology.

3) Consolidation and Refinancing: In some cases, consolidating multiple debts into a single loan or refinancing existing loans can lower interest rates and simplify payments.

4) Emergency Fund: Building an emergency fund can help prevent relying on credit during unexpected financial challenges, reducing the risk of accruing more debt.

5) Seek Professional Help: If you're struggling with debt, consider consulting a credit counselor or financial advisor. They can provide guidance tailored to your situation.

Avoiding Debt Traps:
To navigate credit and debt successfully, be aware of potential pitfalls:

1) Predatory Lending: Be cautious of lenders offering high-interest loans or credit cards with hidden fees. Read terms carefully before committing.

2) Minimum Payments: Making only minimum payments on credit cards can lead to a cycle of debt, as most of your payment goes towards interest rather than reducing the principal.

3) Using Credit for Non-Essentials: Avoid using credit for discretionary purchases that you can't afford to pay off in the near term.

4) Ignoring Warning Signs: If you're consistently struggling to make payments, it's important to address the issue proactively rather than letting it escalate.

In conclusion, navigating credit and debt involves understanding credit concepts, using credit wisely, managing debt effectively, and avoiding common traps. Responsible credit use and prudent debt management are crucial for achieving financial stability and long-term success. Regularly educating yourself about personal finance and seeking professional advice when needed can contribute to your overall financial well-being.

CHAPTER SIX

UNDERSTANDING CREDIT SCORES AND REPORTS

Understanding credit scores and reports is crucial for managing your financial health and making informed decisions about credit-related matters. Credit scores are numerical representations of an individual's creditworthiness, indicating how likely they are to repay borrowed money. Credit reports, on the other hand, are detailed records of a person's credit history and financial behavior. Let's delve into these concepts more deeply:

Credit Scores:

1) Calculation: Credit scores are typically calculated using a mathematical formula that evaluates various aspects of your credit history. Commonly used scoring models include FICO (Fair Isaac Corporation) Score and VantageScore. Factors like payment history, credit utilization, length of credit history, types of credit, and recent credit inquiries influence these scores.

2) Range and Interpretation: FICO Scores range from 300 to 850, with higher scores indicating better creditworthiness. Generally, scores above 700 are considered good, while those above 800 are excellent. Lower scores might result in difficulties obtaining loans or credit at favorable terms.

3) Influencing Factors: Payment history (whether you've paid your bills on time), credit utilization (how much of your available credit you're using), length of credit history, types of credit (credit cards, mortgages,

etc.), and recent credit inquiries impact your score. A history of late payments or high credit card balances can lower your score.

4) Importance: Credit scores are used by lenders to assess your risk as a borrower. They play a significant role in determining whether you qualify for credit, the interest rates you'll receive, and the credit limits you'll be granted.

Credit Reports:

1) Credit reports are compiled by credit bureaus (Equifax, Experian, and TransUnion) based on data provided by creditors, lenders, and public records. They contain detailed information about your credit history, including credit accounts, payment history, balances, and more.

2) Sections: Credit reports consist of sections such as personal information (name, address, etc.), credit accounts (credit cards, loans, mortgages), payment history (on-time and late payments), credit inquiries (requests for your credit report), and public records (bankruptcies, tax liens).

3) Regular Review: It's advisable to review your credit reports regularly to identify errors, inaccuracies, or fraudulent activity. Under the Fair Credit Reporting Act (FCRA), you're entitled to a free credit report from each bureau annually, which you can request from annualcreditreport.com.

4) Disputes and Corrections: If you find errors in your credit report, you can dispute them with the credit bureau. This process can help improve your credit score if errors are resolved.

In essence, understanding credit scores and reports empowers you to manage your finances effectively. By maintaining a good credit history, you can qualify for better loan terms, lower interest rates, and access to various financial opportunities. Regular monitoring of your credit reports ensures the accuracy of the information being used to calculate your credit score. This, in turn, enables you to take steps to improve your credit standing and achieve your financial goals.

TACKLING DEBT AND AVOIDING HIGH-INTEREST TRAPS

Tackling debt and avoiding high-interest traps are essential financial skills that can have a profound impact on one's financial well-being. Whether you're dealing with existing debt or striving to prevent future debt, here are some strategies to consider:

Tackling Debt:

1) Assessment and Prioritization: Start by gathering all your debt information, including balances, interest rates, and minimum payments. Categorize your debts as high-interest (credit cards, payday loans) or low-interest (mortgage, student loans). Prioritize paying off high-interest debts first.

2) Generate a Budget: Construct an all-inclusive budget detailing your earnings and costs. This enables you to pinpoint places for reducing expenses and channeling extra funds towards paying off debts.

Debt Repayment Strategies:

1) Snowball Method: Pay the minimum on all debts except the smallest one. Put extra money towards the smallest debt until it's paid off, then move to the next smallest. This method offers psychological motivation as you see debts being cleared.

2) Avalanche Strategy: Begin by focusing on repaying the debt with the highest interest rate. This approach minimizes long-term costs by decreasing total interest payments.

3) Consolidating Debt: Think about combining high-interest debts into one loan with a lower interest rate. This can enhance affordability and lead to interest savings.

4) Negotiate with Creditors: If you're struggling to make payments, contact your creditors to discuss options. They might be willing to negotiate a lower interest rate or a more manageable repayment plan.

5) Side Hustles and Extra Income: Explore opportunities to increase your income through part-time jobs, freelancing, or selling items you no longer need. The extra funds can be directed towards debt repayment.

Avoiding High-Interest Traps:

1) Emergency Fund: Build an emergency fund to cover unexpected expenses. Having this safety net can prevent you from resorting to high-interest loans or credit cards in times of crisis.

2) Utilizing Credit Cards Wisely: While credit cards offer convenience, they frequently entail steep interest charges. To prevent accruing interest, make sure to settle your credit card dues entirely every month. If you do maintain a balance, explore cards featuring lower interest rates.

3) Research and Compare: Before taking on any form of debt, research different options and compare interest rates and terms. This applies to loans, credit cards, and any financial products you're considering.

4) Avoid Payday Loans: These short-term, high-interest loans can quickly trap you in a cycle of debt. Explore alternatives such as borrowing from family or friends, negotiating with creditors, or seeking assistance from non-profit credit counseling agencies.

5) Educate Yourself: Understand how interest works, how different types of loans function, and the implications of missing payments. Financial literacy is a powerful tool in avoiding high-interest debt traps.

6) Embrace Financial Prudence: Steer clear of the urge to overspend or adopt a lifestyle that surpasses your financial capabilities. Foster disciplined expenditure habits and prioritize saving over avoidable outlays.

7) Invest in Yourself: Consider investing in education or skills that can increase your earning potential. This can help you avoid financial struggles in the long run.

Tackling debt and avoiding high-interest traps require discipline, careful planning, and a willingness to make necessary lifestyle changes. By implementing these strategies, you can regain control of your finances and work towards a more secure and debt-free future.

BUILDING A SUPPORTIVE FINANCIAL ENVIRONMENT

Building a supportive financial environment involves creating conditions that promote financial stability, growth, and well-being for individuals, families, businesses, and communities. This encompasses a range of factors, from government policies and regulations to personal financial education and cultural attitudes towards money. Here's an in-depth exploration of the key components and strategies to achieve a supportive financial environment:

1) Policy and Regulation: Regulations that ensure consumer protection, fair lending practices, and financial transparency are essential. For example, enforcing regulations that prevent predatory lending or fraudulent financial schemes helps create a safer environment for financial transactions.

2) Access to Financial Services:
A supportive financial environment ensures that individuals and businesses have access to a range of financial services, including banking, credit, insurance, and investment opportunities. Efforts to promote financial inclusion, especially among marginalized communities, can lead to improved economic outcomes.

3) Financial Literacy and Education:
Educating individuals about personal finance and money management is pivotal. Schools, workplaces, and community organizations can offer

financial literacy programs to teach skills like budgeting, saving,
investing, and debt management.

4) Savings and Investment Incentives:
Governments and institutions can provide incentives to encourage
saving and investing. Tax benefits for retirement contributions,
matching funds for savings, and grants for business investments can
motivate people to secure their financial futures.

5) Support for Entrepreneurs and Small Businesses:
A favorable environment for entrepreneurs and small businesses is
essential for economic growth. Access to affordable loans, business
development resources, and mentorship programs can help these
ventures thrive.

6) Consumer Protection and Financial Stability:
Financial crises can have far-reaching impacts. Regulatory measures and
institutions that ensure the stability of financial markets, protect
consumers from unfair practices, and regulate systemic risks are critical
for maintaining a supportive environment.

7) Cultural Attitudes Towards Money:
Societal attitudes towards money influence financial behaviors.
Encouraging a culture of responsible spending, saving, and investment
can foster a healthier financial environment. This can involve changing
perceptions about debt, savings, and long-term planning.

8) Technological Innovation:
Technological advancements have transformed financial services.
Fintech solutions like mobile banking, digital wallets, and investment
apps have increased access and convenience. Embracing innovation can
enhance financial inclusion and efficiency.

9) Supportive Workplace Policies:
Employers can contribute to a supportive financial environment by
offering benefits like retirement plans, financial counseling, and flexible
savings accounts. These initiatives help employees manage their finances
effectively.

10) Social Safety Nets:
Comprehensive social safety nets, including unemployment benefits, healthcare coverage, and housing assistance, provide a safety net during difficult financial times, reducing the likelihood of individuals falling into severe financial distress.

11) Collaboration and Partnerships:
Building a supportive financial environment requires collaboration among governments, financial institutions, educational institutions, nonprofits, and businesses. Partnerships can leverage diverse expertise to create comprehensive strategies.

12) Long-Term Vision and Adaptability:
A sustainable financial environment requires a long-term perspective and adaptability to changing economic conditions. Continuously evaluating policies and strategies and making necessary adjustments is crucial for ongoing success.

In summary, building a supportive financial environment involves a multifaceted approach that addresses policy, education, access, culture, and innovation. By prioritizing financial education, responsible lending practices, and inclusive policies, societies can work toward creating an environment where financial stability and prosperity are attainable for all.

CHAPTER SEVEN

COMMUNICATING WITH FAMILY AND FRIENDS ABOUT MONEY

Communicating about money with family and friends is a vital aspect of maintaining healthy relationships and managing financial matters effectively. Open and transparent discussions can help prevent misunderstandings, reduce conflicts, and ensure everyone involved is on the same page. Here are some key points to consider when communicating about money:

1) Choose the Right Time and Place: Select a neutral and comfortable environment for discussions about money. Avoid bringing up financial topics during stressful moments or when emotions are running high.

2) Be Honest and Open: Honesty is crucial when discussing money matters. Share your financial situation, goals, and concerns openly. Transparency fosters trust and encourages others to reciprocate.

3) Set Clear Boundaries: Clearly define what topics are open for discussion and what should remain private. This prevents overstepping boundaries and maintains a respectful atmosphere.

4) Active Listening: Pay attention to what others are saying without interruption. Listen to their perspectives, needs, and concerns before expressing your own opinions.

5) Avoid Judgment: When discussing money, it's important to refrain from being judgmental or critical. People have different financial situations and goals, and empathy goes a long way in maintaining strong relationships.

6) Discuss Shared Goals: If you have shared financial goals, such as planning a vacation or buying a property together, discuss them openly. This helps align everyone's efforts and ensures everyone is committed to the same objectives.

7) Respect Differences: Understand that people have different financial priorities and beliefs. What may seem important to you might not hold the same significance for others. Respect these differences to avoid conflicts.

8) Be Patient: Financial conversations can be complex and emotional. Be patient, especially if the topic is sensitive. Give others time to process information and express their thoughts.

9) Avoid Blame: Rather than blaming or pointing fingers, focus on finding solutions together. If mistakes were made, approach them as learning experiences and opportunities for growth.

10) Seek Professional Advice: In some situations, it might be helpful to involve a financial advisor or planner. Their expertise can provide objective insights and help mediate discussions.

11) Regular Check-Ins: Make discussing money a regular part of your conversations, especially if you share financial responsibilities. Regular check-ins can help identify issues early and adjust plans accordingly.

12) Be Prepared for Change: Financial situations can change over time due to various reasons. Be prepared to adapt and modify plans as needed, and communicate these changes to your family and friends.

13) Celebrate Achievements: Celebrate financial milestones and achievements together. This reinforces positive behaviors and encourages everyone to stay focused on their goals.

Remember, effective communication about money requires ongoing effort and a willingness to work together. By creating an environment of trust and understanding, you can navigate financial discussions with your family and friends successfully.

SEEKING PROFESSIONAL FINANCIAL ADVICE

Seeking professional financial advice is a critical step toward achieving your financial goals and ensuring your long-term financial well-being. While it might be tempting to manage your finances on your own, a skilled financial advisor can provide you with expert guidance, tailored strategies, and a comprehensive understanding of complex financial matters.

Here are some key points to consider when seeking professional financial advice:

1) Expertise and Knowledge: Financial advisors possess a deep understanding of various financial concepts, including investment strategies, tax planning, retirement planning, estate planning, risk management, and more. Their knowledge helps them analyze your unique financial situation and develop suitable recommendations.

2) Personalized Approach: A good financial advisor takes the time to understand your specific goals, risk tolerance, time horizon, and current financial situation. This enables them to create a personalized financial plan that aligns with your objectives.

3) Objective Perspective: Emotional biases can often cloud our judgement when making financial decisions. A financial advisor provides an objective viewpoint and helps you make rational choices based on facts and analysis rather than emotions.

4) Comprehensive Financial Planning: Financial advisors help you create a holistic financial plan that considers all aspects of your financial life, from budgeting and saving to investing and retirement planning. This comprehensive approach ensures that no critical elements are overlooked.

5) Investment Guidance: Navigating the world of investments can be complex and overwhelming. A financial advisor can help you design an investment portfolio that matches your risk tolerance, financial goals, and time horizon. They monitor the portfolio's performance and make adjustments as needed.

6) Risk Management: Financial advisors can assess your risk exposure and recommend strategies to mitigate potential risks. This could include insurance coverage, emergency funds, and diversification in investments.

7) Tax Efficiency: A financial advisor can help you optimize your tax strategy by identifying tax-saving opportunities, managing tax implications of investments, and suggesting tax-efficient investment vehicles.

8) Retirement Planning: Planning for retirement involves careful consideration of factors such as savings, investment returns, Social Security, and more. A financial advisor can help you determine how much you need to save and invest to maintain your desired lifestyle in retirement.

9) Estate Planning: If you have significant assets, an estate plan is crucial for ensuring a smooth transfer of wealth to your heirs while minimizing taxes and legal complications. A financial advisor can work with estate planning attorneys to develop an effective strategy.

10) Continuous Monitoring and Adjustments: Financial markets and personal circumstances can change over time. A financial advisor regularly reviews your financial plan, makes necessary adjustments, and keeps you on track toward your goals.

11) Credentials and Regulation: When choosing a financial advisor, look for credentials such as Certified Financial Planner (CFP), Chartered Financial Analyst (CFA), or Certified Public Accountant (CPA). Additionally, ensure that the advisor is registered with appropriate regulatory bodies to maintain ethical and professional standards.

12) Fees and Compensation: Different advisors have various fee structures, including commission-based, fee-only, or a combination. It's important to understand how your advisor is compensated and to clarify any potential conflicts of interest.

In conclusion, seeking professional financial advice is a prudent step to take control of your financial future. A qualified financial advisor can offer valuable insights, create a tailored financial plan, and help you navigate the complexities of financial decision-making, ultimately increasing your chances of achieving your financial goals.

CHAPTER EIGHT

SUSTAINING POSITIVE CHANGE

Sustaining positive change involves the continued maintenance and reinforcement of beneficial modifications in various aspects of life, whether they are personal, societal, or organizational. Achieving positive change is a significant accomplishment, but ensuring its continuity over the long term can be just as challenging. Here are some key factors and strategies to consider when aiming to sustain positive change:

1) Clear Goals and Vision: Having a clear understanding of the desired outcome is essential. Whether it's improving one's health, promoting environmental sustainability, or enhancing workplace culture, a well-defined vision provides direction and motivation for the change effort.

2) Gradual Implementation: Rushing change can lead to burnout and resistance. Gradually introducing modifications allows individuals and systems to adapt and integrate the changes into their routines, increasing the likelihood of long-term success.

3) Behavioral Reinforcement: Positive change often involves altering behaviors. Employ strategies like positive reinforcement, rewards, and recognition to encourage the continuation of new habits and actions.

4) Education and Awareness: Keep stakeholders informed about the benefits of the change and the progress made. By understanding the positive impact, individuals are more likely to remain engaged and committed to sustaining the change.

5) Measurement and Evaluation: Regularly track and measure the progress of the change initiative. Collect data on key performance indicators to assess the impact and identify areas that require adjustment.

6) Adaptability: Circumstances may change over time, and flexibility is crucial. Be prepared to adapt strategies and approaches to fit evolving needs and challenges.

7) Leadership and Role Modeling: Strong leadership sets the tone for sustaining positive change. Leaders should consistently demonstrate the desired behaviors and actively support the change effort to inspire others.

8) Cultural Integration: Embed the change within the culture of the organization or community. When the change becomes part of the norm, it is more likely to be sustained.

9) Community and Peer Support: Establish a supportive environment where individuals can share their experiences, challenges, and successes. Peer support and community involvement create a sense of accountability and camaraderie.

10) Communication: Maintain open and transparent communication channels. Address concerns, answer questions, and provide updates regularly to keep stakeholders engaged and informed.

11) Training and Skill Development: Equip individuals with the necessary skills and knowledge to sustain the change. Training programs can empower people to continue practicing new behaviors effectively.

12) Celebrate Milestones: Celebrate achievements along the way. Acknowledging progress reinforces the positive impact of the change effort and boosts morale.

13) Long-Term Perspective: Sustaining positive change requires a long-term perspective. Acknowledge that setbacks may occur, but focus

on learning from them and continuing the journey toward the desired outcome.

14) Data-Driven Approach: Use data and feedback to make informed decisions about adjustments and improvements. Regular analysis of data can help identify trends and areas that need further attention.

15) Institutionalization: If possible, integrate the change into policies, procedures, and structures to ensure its longevity even as personnel or leadership changes.

Ultimately, sustaining positive change is a dynamic process that requires ongoing effort, dedication, and a holistic approach. By addressing various factors and adopting appropriate strategies, individuals and organizations can increase the likelihood of maintaining the positive changes they have worked hard to achieve.

DEALING WITH SETBACKS AND STAYING MOTIVATED

Dealing with setbacks and staying motivated are essential skills for navigating the ups and downs of life. Setbacks are inevitable, but how you respond to them can greatly impact your overall success and well-being. Here's an extensive overview of strategies to effectively handle setbacks and maintain motivation:

1. Embrace Resilience:
Resilience entails the capacity to rebound from challenges. Foster this quality by recognizing your emotions while also reframing difficulties as chances for personal growth. Recognize that setbacks are a normal part of any journey and can yield valuable insights.

2. Maintain Perspective:
When setbacks occur, it's easy to lose sight of the bigger picture. Remind yourself of your long-term goals and how this setback fits into the grand

scheme of things. Often, setbacks are just temporary roadblocks on your path to success.

3. Learn from Failure:
Regard setbacks as opportunities for learning. Evaluate what went awry and pinpoint lessons that can be carried forward into future undertakings. Failure serves as a stepping stone to success; numerous accomplished individuals have encountered multiple failures prior to attaining their objectives.

4. Set Realistic Expectations:
Unrealistic expectations can lead to disappointment and demotivation. Set achievable goals that challenge you without overwhelming your capabilities. This way, even if setbacks occur, they won't derail your entire motivation.

5. Break Down Goals:
Large goals can feel overwhelming, making setbacks seem insurmountable. Break down your goals into smaller, manageable tasks. This allows you to focus on incremental progress and celebrate small victories along the way.

6. Practice Self-Compassion:
Extend kindness to yourself during setbacks. Steer clear of self-blame and pessimistic self-dialogue. Offer yourself the same empathy and comprehension that you would extend to a friend grappling with a similar situation.

7. Seek Support:
Don't be afraid to reach out for support from friends, family, mentors, or professionals. Sharing your feelings and experiences can help alleviate stress and provide fresh perspectives on how to overcome setbacks.

8. Adapt and Pivot:

Setbacks often require adapting to new circumstances. Be open to adjusting your approach or trying new strategies. Flexibility and adaptability are key traits in overcoming obstacles.

9. Visualization and Affirmations:
Visualizing success and using positive affirmations can help maintain motivation during challenging times. Envisioning your desired outcome can keep you focused on the end goal, even when setbacks arise.

10. Stay Consistent:
Consistency is crucial for maintaining motivation. Establish routines that keep you engaged with your goals, even when setbacks occur. Consistency helps you stay connected to your aspirations and prevents demotivation.

11. Celebrate Progress:
Admit and rejoice in your accomplishments, regardless of their scale. Acknowledging your advancements, even when facing setbacks, reinforces a constructive mindset and enhances motivation.

12. Practice Mindfulness:
Mindfulness techniques, such as meditation and deep breathing, can help manage stress and anxiety caused by setbacks. Being present in the moment can reduce negative thoughts and help you refocus on your goals.

13. Find Inspiration:
Seek inspiration from various sources, such as books, podcasts, or role models. Learning about others' journeys and how they overcame setbacks can provide a fresh perspective on your own challenges.

14. Setbacks as Feedback:
View setbacks as feedback on your approach rather than personal failures. This shift in mindset allows you to identify areas for improvement and adjust your strategies accordingly.

15. Focus on What You Can Control:

While you can't control every aspect of a situation, you can control your response and actions. Direct your energy toward things you can influence, and let go of factors beyond your control.

In summary, setbacks are a natural part of life, and staying motivated through challenges requires a combination of resilience, perspective, and adaptive strategies. By cultivating these skills and maintaining a positive outlook, you can navigate setbacks with grace and continue progressing toward your goals.

CELEBRATING MILESTONES AND ACHIEVEMENT

Celebrating milestones and achievements holds a significant place in human culture and psychology. These events mark important moments of progress, growth, and success, providing individuals and communities with a sense of accomplishment and motivation. Whether it's a personal achievement like graduating from school, a professional milestone such as completing a project, or a collective accomplishment like reaching a company's annual goal, celebrating these moments has various positive impacts.

1) Recognition and Validation: Celebrations acknowledge the efforts and hard work that have gone into reaching a goal. They provide individuals with validation for their dedication, perseverance, and commitment. This recognition fosters a sense of pride and boosts self-esteem, encouraging individuals to continue striving for excellence.

2) Motivation and Inspiration: Celebrating milestones and achievements serves as a source of motivation and inspiration for both the person accomplishing the feat and those around them. Sharing success stories and acknowledging progress can motivate others to set their own goals and work towards them with determination.

3) Positive Reinforcement: Positive reinforcement plays a vital role in behavior psychology. Celebrating achievements reinforces the behavior

and actions that led to success, making it more likely for individuals to repeat those actions in the future.

4) Building a Positive Culture: In organizations, celebrating achievements contributes to creating a positive and collaborative work culture. It fosters a sense of camaraderie and team spirit, encouraging employees to support one another's success and collaborate effectively.

5) Marking Milestones of Growth: Personal and professional growth is often marked by milestones and achievements. Celebrating these moments allows individuals to reflect on their journey, from where they started to where they are now. This reflection can be a source of personal satisfaction and motivation to continue evolving.

6) Strengthening Relationships: Celebrations bring people together, whether it's a family gathering for a graduation or a team celebrating a project's successful completion. These events provide opportunities for bonding, networking, and forming deeper connections with others who share in the joy of the achievement.

7) Creating Lasting Memories: Special occasions like milestone celebrations create cherished memories that individuals can look back on with fondness. These memories often serve as reminders of the progress made and the hurdles overcome, serving as a source of inspiration during challenging times.

8) Promoting Goal Setting: Celebrating achievements encourages individuals to set new goals and pursue further growth. By reflecting on what they've accomplished, individuals can identify areas for improvement and set higher aspirations.

9) Boosting Overall Well-being: Celebrations trigger the release of dopamine, a neurotransmitter associated with pleasure and reward. This leads to an overall positive impact on mental and emotional well-being, contributing to reduced stress and enhanced happiness.

10) Cultural and Social Significance: Celebrating milestones is deeply ingrained in human culture and tradition. These celebrations often have

cultural, religious, or social significance, enriching the tapestry of human experience and connecting people across time and geography.

In conclusion, celebrating milestones and achievements is more than just a moment of revelry. It's a way to acknowledge hard work, inspire others, reinforce positive behaviors, and build a sense of community. By recognizing and commemorating these significant moments, individuals and groups can derive a multitude of psychological, social, and emotional benefits that contribute to their personal and collective growth.

CHAPTER NINE

CASE STUDIES: REAL-LIFE TRANSFORMATIONS

Real-life case studies are powerful examples of how organizations or individuals have undergone significant transformations to overcome challenges, achieve goals, or adapt to changing circumstances. These case studies provide valuable insights into the strategies, tactics, and approaches employed to drive successful change. Here are a few notable examples of real-life transformations:

1) Netflix's Evolution: Netflix began as a DVD rental-by-mail service but underwent a massive transformation into a streaming media powerhouse. By recognizing the shift in consumer behavior towards digital content consumption, Netflix shifted its focus towards online streaming. This strategic transformation not only changed the way people watch TV shows and movies but also disrupted the traditional entertainment industry.

2) Apple's Resurgence: In the late 1990s, Apple was struggling financially and facing fierce competition. Steve Jobs returned to the company and orchestrated a remarkable transformation. Apple shifted its focus from a niche computer manufacturer to a consumer electronics and software giant. The introduction of the iPod, followed by the iPhone and iPad, catapulted Apple to become one of the most valuable companies in the world.

3) Starbucks' Global Expansion: Starbucks began as a single coffee shop in Seattle. Through careful branding, customer experience, and

innovative store concepts, it successfully expanded into a global coffeehouse chain. Starbucks' transformation wasn't just about selling coffee; it was about selling an experience, a "third place" between work and home.

4) LEGO's Turnaround: In the early 2000s, LEGO was on the brink of bankruptcy due to financial mismanagement and competition from digital entertainment. By returning to its core values of creative play and interlocking bricks, LEGO transformed itself into a toy and media company with a strong focus on imagination and innovation.

5) Domino's Pizza Reinvention: Domino's faced criticism for the quality of its pizzas. In response, the company launched an ambitious transformation campaign, admitting its shortcomings and pledging to improve. Through innovative recipes, transparency, and a renewed commitment to customer feedback, Domino's turned its negative reputation around and experienced a significant increase in sales.

6) Amazon's Growth Strategy: Amazon started as an online bookstore but quickly transformed into a global e-commerce giant. Over time, it expanded its offerings to include cloud computing services (Amazon Web Services), digital streaming (Amazon Prime Video), smart devices (Amazon Echo), and more. Amazon's focus on customer-centricity and relentless innovation drove its transformation and market dominance.

7) Tesla's Electric Revolution: Tesla disrupted the automotive industry by transforming electric cars from a niche concept to a desirable and innovative product. Through cutting-edge technology, sleek designs, and a commitment to sustainable transportation, Tesla has spurred other automakers to invest heavily in electric vehicle development.

8) McDonald's Healthier Menu: Responding to changing consumer preferences, McDonald's underwent a transformation by introducing healthier menu options, reducing trans fats, and offering more transparency about nutritional information. This move aimed to address concerns about fast food's impact on health and nutrition.

Real-life case studies like these offer valuable lessons for businesses and individuals looking to navigate change and achieve growth. They showcase the importance of adaptability, innovation, customer-centricity, and strategic planning in the face of challenges and evolving market landscapes. By analyzing these transformations, stakeholders can gain insights into the strategies and approaches that drive successful change initiatives.

STORIES OF INDIVIDUALS WHO OVERCAME POOR MONEY HABITS

Certainly! Stories of individuals who have overcome poor money habits can be incredibly inspiring and serve as examples for others looking to improve their financial situations. Here are a few noteworthy examples:

1) Dave Ramsey: Dave Ramsey is a well-known personal finance expert who went from bankruptcy to financial success. He accumulated significant debt in his early adult life but managed to turn his life around by adopting a strict budget, cutting unnecessary expenses, and using the "snowball method" to pay off his debts. He has since become a renowned author, radio host, and speaker, helping millions of people achieve financial independence.

2) Suze Orman: Suze Orman grew up with very little financial education and made several poor money decisions in her early years. However, she managed to turn her life around by learning about personal finance and investing. She worked as a waitress and saved aggressively to start her own business. Today, she is a best-selling author and a respected financial advisor, helping others take control of their finances.

3) Trent Hamm: Trent Hamm is the founder of "The Simple Dollar," a popular personal finance blog. He struggled with excessive spending, credit card debt, and poor financial decisions. Through research and determination, he learned how to live frugally, pay off his debts, and

manage his finances wisely. He now shares his experiences and insights on his blog, helping others make positive changes in their financial lives.

4) Elizabeth Warren: Before becoming a U.S. Senator and a prominent figure in American politics, Elizabeth Warren faced personal financial challenges. As a young mother, she dealt with job loss and financial instability. She went on to pursue education and eventually became a law professor. Her experiences with financial difficulties led her to research and advocate for better consumer protection laws and financial regulation.

5) Chris Hogan: Chris Hogan, a former football player and now a financial coach, struggled with debt and poor money habits early in his career. He managed to eliminate his debt and establish a strong financial foundation by following a disciplined plan, living below his means, and making wise investment choices. He now helps individuals achieve their financial goals through coaching, speaking engagements, and his books.

These stories emphasize the importance of determination, education, and making intentional choices when it comes to managing money. They demonstrate that with the right mindset and strategies, anyone can overcome poor money habits and achieve financial success.

CONCLUSION

EMBRACING A FUTURE OF FINANCIAL WELL-WELL-BEING

Embracing a future of financial well-being is a pivotal aspect of leading a fulfilling and balanced life. It involves a proactive and mindful approach to managing one's finances, ensuring stability, freedom, and the ability to pursue one's goals and dreams. This concept encompasses a variety of principles and practices that contribute to a strong financial foundation.

1.   Financial Literacy: The first step towards achieving financial well-being is acquiring knowledge about financial concepts, such as budgeting, saving, investing, and debt management. Being financially literate empowers individuals to make informed decisions and avoid pitfalls that can lead to financial stress.

2.   Goal Setting: Setting clear financial goals is crucial. Whether it's buying a home, funding education, starting a business, or retiring comfortably, having well-defined objectives provides direction and motivation for managing money effectively.

3.   Budgeting: Creating and adhering to a budget is fundamental. It helps track income and expenses, identify areas for improvement, and ensure that money is allocated appropriately to meet various needs and desires.

4.   Emergency Fund: Establishing an emergency fund acts as a safety net during unexpected financial setbacks, such as medical expenses, job

loss, or major repairs. An often given suggestion is to set aside enough money to cover living expenses for three to six months.

5.   Debt Management: Responsible management of debt involves minimizing high-interest debt and paying it off systematically. This can relieve financial stress and free up resources for other important goals.

6.   Saving and Investing: Regular saving and investing enable the growth of wealth over time. Diversifying with long-term goals are key components of this aspect.

7.   Retirement Planning: Planning for retirement ensures a comfortable and secure future. Contributing to retirement accounts, such as 401(k)s or IRAs, can help build a nest egg that provides financial freedom during one's golden years.

8.   Mindful Spending: Being mindful of spending habits encourages responsible consumption. Prioritizing needs over wants and making intentional spending choices can prevent unnecessary financial strain.

9.   Continuous Learning: The financial landscape is constantly evolving. Staying updated on market trends, investment options, and new financial tools can help individuals make well-informed decisions.

10.   Seek Professional Advice: Consulting with financial advisors or experts can provide personalized guidance tailored to individual circumstances. They can help create customized financial plans and strategies to achieve specific goals.

11.   Psychological Well-being: Financial well-being is not solely about numbers; it also involves psychological and emotional factors. Reducing financial stress and anxiety contributes to overall well-being.

12.   Generosity and Giving: Embracing financial well-being can also include contributing to causes and helping others in need. Acts of

generosity and charitable giving can provide a sense of purpose and fulfillment.

13.   Adaptability: Life is full of unexpected changes. Embracing financial well-being involves being adaptable and having contingency plans to navigate through challenges and seize opportunities.

In conclusion, embracing a future of financial well-being requires a holistic approach that combines knowledge, discipline, and adaptability. It's about creating a solid financial foundation that supports personal and professional aspirations, while also contributing to overall happiness and contentment. By adopting these principles and practices, individuals can work towards a more secure and fulfilling financial future.

INTRODUCTIONS
UNDERSTANDING THE IMPACT OF POOR MONEY HABITS

poor money habits can have far-reaching consequences that affect
various aspects of our lives. these habits can create a cycle of financial
stress and instability, impacting our present and future financial
well-being. here are some key points to consider when examining the
impact of poor money habits:

1) debt accumulation: one of the most common consequences of poor
money habits is the accumulation of debt. overspending, relying on
credit cards, and living beyond one's means can lead to high-interest
debt that becomes difficult to manage. this debt not only affects your
credit score but also limits your financial freedom and future
opportunities.

2) limited savings: poor money management often leads to inadequate
savings. without a proper savings strategy, you might struggle to cover
unexpected expenses, emergencies, or future goals such as buying a
house, funding education, or retiring comfortably. this lack of savings
can perpetuate a cycle of financial instability.

3) stress and mental health: financial stress resulting from poor money
habits can negatively impact mental health. constantly worrying about
bills, debt payments, and financial obligations can lead to anxiety,

depression, and decreased overall well-being. this stress can also affect
personal relationships and work performance.

4) missed investment opportunities: failing to invest wisely due to poor
money habits can result in missed opportunities for wealth accumulation
and financial growth. delaying or neglecting investment planning can
hinder your ability to build wealth over time, potentially affecting your
long-term financial security.

5) inadequate retirement planning: poor money habits can lead to
inadequate retirement planning. failing to contribute to retirement
accounts and not prioritizing long-term financial goals can leave you
ill-prepared for retirement, forcing you to work longer than desired or
compromising your lifestyle in your later years.

6) lack of financial literacy: poor money habits often stem from a lack of
financial literacy. without understanding basic financial concepts such as
budgeting, saving, investing, and managing credit, individuals are more
likely to make poor financial decisions that impact their financial
stability.

7) impact on relationships: financial disagreements are a common
source of conflict in relationships. poor money habits can strain
partnerships, marriages, and family relationships due to disagreements
over spending, saving, and financial goals.

8) opportunity cost: poor money habits also come with opportunity
costs. money spent on frivolous purchases or unnecessary expenses
could have been used for more meaningful purposes, such as
experiences, education, or investments that contribute to personal
growth and financial stability.

9) cyclical nature: poor money habits can create a cycle that's difficult to
break. people who consistently make poor financial decisions might find
themselves trapped in a pattern of debt and financial instability, making
it challenging to improve their situation.

10) long-term financial goals: poor money habits can significantly hinder the achievement of long-term financial goals. whether it's buying a home, starting a business, or traveling, these goals require careful financial planning and discipline. poor money habits can delay or even prevent the realization of such aspirations.

in conclusion, understanding the impact of poor money habits is crucial for maintaining financial well-being. by recognizing the consequences these habits can have on debt, savings, mental health, relationships, and long-term goals, individuals can take proactive steps to improve their financial habits. this includes educating themselves about financial literacy, creating a budget, managing debt responsibly, saving consistently, and seeking professional guidance when needed. by making positive changes to their money habits, individuals can pave the way for a more secure and fulfilling financial future.

THE PSYCHOLOGY OF MONEY HABITS

the psychology of money habits is a fascinating area of study that delves into the complex interplay between human behavior, financial decision-making, and long-term financial well-being. our habits surrounding money are deeply rooted in psychological, emotional, and cognitive factors. here are some key points to consider:

1) behavioral economics: the field of behavioral economics explores how psychological factors influence economic decisions. it highlights that humans often don't make rational decisions, but instead are influenced by cognitive biases, emotions, and social pressures. this has a significant impact on how we handle money.

2) emotional triggers: money is not just a tool; it carries emotional weight. people often associate money with security, success, power, and even self-worth. these emotional associations can drive both positive and negative money habits. for example, emotional spending or retail therapy can be a result of seeking comfort or happiness through purchases.

3) herd mentality: people are highly influenced by the behavior of others, especially in financial matters. this can lead to herd mentality, where individuals make financial decisions based on the actions of those around them, rather than independent analysis. herd behavior can result in bubbles in financial markets or unnecessary expenses.

4) delayed gratification: the ability to delay gratification is a key predictor of financial success. individuals who can resist immediate rewards in favor of long-term goals tend to have healthier money habits. this trait is linked to self-control and the capacity to manage impulsive spending.

5) anchoring and framing: the way information is presented or framed can greatly impact financial decisions. anchoring refers to the tendency to rely heavily on the first piece of information encountered when making decisions, while framing involves how options are presented. these cognitive biases can influence perceptions of value and impact spending choices.

6) loss aversion: the fear of loss is a powerful motivator. people often go to great lengths to avoid losses, even if it means making irrational decisions. this can lead to holding onto losing investments, refusing to cut losses, and avoiding risks that might be beneficial.

7) money personality types: different individuals have different money personalities. some are savers, some are spenders, and others are risk-takers. understanding your own money personality can help you make more aligned financial choices and develop healthier money habits.

8) financial childhood experiences: early experiences with money, including how it was discussed and managed in the family, can shape an individual's financial behavior in adulthood. for instance, growing up in an environment of scarcity or overspending can influence one's relationship with money.

9) automated decision-making: creating automated systems for saving, investing, and bill payments can mitigate the impact of impulsive

decisions. by setting up these systems, individuals can take advantage of their cognitive biases, such as inertia, to foster positive money habits.

10) behavioral interventions: researchers and experts have developed various strategies to help individuals improve their money habits. these interventions often involve setting specific goals, creating visual cues, and implementing accountability mechanisms to encourage positive financial behavior.

in conclusion, the psychology of money habits is a multidimensional subject that encompasses cognitive biases, emotions, social influences, and past experiences. by understanding these factors, individuals can work toward cultivating healthier money habits and achieving greater financial well-being.

CHAPTER ONE

UNCOVERING THE ROOT CAUSES OF FINANCIAL MISSTEPS

uncovering the root causes of financial missteps is essential for individuals, businesses, and even governments to understand and mitigate the risks associated with poor financial decision-making. financial missteps can encompass a wide range of errors, including overspending, poor investment choices, debt accumulation, and failure to plan for the future. identifying these root causes can help prevent such mistakes from happening and enable better financial management. here are some key aspects to consider when delving into the root causes of financial missteps:

1) lack of financial literacy: one of the primary reasons for financial missteps is a lack of understanding of basic financial concepts. many individuals and even businesses struggle with financial literacy, which can lead to uninformed decisions, misunderstandings about interest rates, loans, and investments, and an overall inability to manage finances effectively.

2) emotional decision-making: emotions can heavily influence financial decisions. fear, greed, and impulsiveness can lead to poor choices.

investors might panic during market downturns, leading them to sell off investments at a loss. similarly, impulsive spending due to emotional triggers can result in accumulating debt.

3) inadequate planning: failure to set clear financial goals and create a comprehensive budget can lead to overspending and inadequate savings. without proper planning, individuals and businesses may not have a clear roadmap for their financial future, making it difficult to make informed decisions.

4) peer pressure and lifestyle inflation: keeping up with the spending habits of friends, family, or colleagues can lead to unnecessary expenditures. this phenomenon, known as lifestyle inflation, can cause individuals to overspend and neglect saving for future needs.

5) risk misperception: misunderstanding or underestimating the risks associated with investments or financial decisions can result in significant losses. this can occur when individuals invest in complex financial products without fully comprehending the associated risks.

6) overconfidence: overestimating one's financial knowledge or investment skills can lead to risky decisions. overconfident individuals may engage in speculative trading or make high-risk investments without proper research.

7) ignoring interest rates: failing to understand the impact of interest rates on loans and credit cards can result in accumulating high levels of debt. ignoring the compounding effect of interest can lead to long-term financial challenges.

8) inadequate emergency fund: not having an emergency fund can make individuals vulnerable to unexpected expenses, leading to the use of credit cards or loans to cover these costs. this can start a cycle of debt.

9) herd mentality: following the crowd without conducting independent research can lead to financial missteps. this is particularly relevant in investment decisions, where herd mentality can cause assets to become overvalued or undervalued.

10) complex financial products: lack of understanding of complex financial instruments, such as derivatives or structured products, can result in significant losses. investments in products with hidden risks can lead to unexpected financial downturns.

11) inadequate risk management: not having insurance coverage or underestimating potential risks, such as health issues or property damage, can lead to financial strain during emergencies.

12) procrastination: delaying financial decisions, such as retirement planning or debt repayment, can result in missed opportunities and increased financial stress over time.

in order to address these root causes and avoid financial missteps, individuals and entities should prioritize financial education, seek professional advice when needed, develop clear financial goals, establish a budget, practice disciplined decision-making, and continuously evaluate and adjust their financial strategies. taking a proactive and informed approach to managing finances can significantly reduce the likelihood of falling victim to common financial pitfalls.

HOW BEHAVIORAL PATTERNS AFFECT YOUR FINANCES

behavioral patterns have a profound impact on one's financial decisions and outcomes. these patterns encompass a wide range of psychological tendencies, biases, and habits that influence how individuals perceive, approach, and manage their finances. understanding these patterns is crucial because they can either lead to financial success or contribute to detrimental outcomes.

1) spending habits: behavioral patterns often determine how individuals spend their money. impulse buying, emotional spending, and conspicuous consumption can lead to overspending, debt accumulation, and an inability to save effectively.

2) delayed gratification: the ability to delay immediate rewards for long-term financial gains is a key behavioral trait. individuals who struggle with delayed gratification may struggle with saving, investing, and achieving financial goals.

3) anchoring and adjustment: people tend to rely heavily on initial pieces of information when making financial decisions. anchoring to a certain price point or value can lead to unrealistic expectations or inappropriate judgments about the value of assets or investments.

4) loss aversion: the fear of loss often drives decisions more than the potential for gain. this can result in individuals holding onto losing investments for too long, missing out on opportunities, or avoiding calculated risks.

5) confirmation bias: people tend to seek information that confirms their existing beliefs and ignore contrary evidence. this can lead to poor investment choices if individuals only seek information that aligns with their preconceived notions.

6) herd mentality: following the crowd without thorough analysis can lead to poor financial decisions. for instance, investing in a particular asset solely because others are doing so can lead to bubbles and crashes.

7) overconfidence: many individuals overestimate their financial knowledge and abilities. this can lead to excessive trading, overestimating investment returns, and making risky decisions.

8) mental accounting: people often categorize money into different mental accounts based on its source or intended use. this can lead to suboptimal decisions, such as treating a windfall differently from regular income.

9) sunk cost fallacy: this refers to the tendency to continue investing in something based on the resources already committed, even if it no longer makes financial sense. it can lead to holding onto failing investments or projects.

10) behavioral biases: numerous cognitive biases, such as availability bias, framing effects, and endowment effect, influence financial choices. these biases can result in suboptimal asset allocation, investment decisions, and risk management.

11) financial goal setting: behavioral patterns play a role in how individuals set and pursue financial goals. setting realistic, achievable goals and breaking them down into smaller steps can help overcome procrastination and improve financial outcomes.

12) budgeting and saving: effective budgeting requires discipline and self-control, which are influenced by behavioral patterns. the ability to allocate funds for different purposes and stick to a budget can impact long-term financial stability.

recognizing these behavioral patterns and actively working to mitigate their negative effects is essential for financial success. techniques such as mindfulness, financial education, seeking advice, and setting up systems that counteract these biases can help individuals make more rational and informed financial decisions.

IDENTIFYING YOUR POOR MONEY HABITS

identifying your poor money habits is a crucial step towards achieving financial stability and success. these habits can significantly impact your financial well-being over time, often leading to debt, limited savings, and stress. here's an extensive guide on how to identify and address your poor money habits:

1) self-awareness: start by recognizing that you may have poor money habits. this requires an honest assessment of your financial behaviors, decisions, and patterns.

2) track your spending: keep a detailed record of every expense for a month or two. categorize your spending to identify where your money is going. this will reveal areas where you might be overspending or making unnecessary purchases.

3) review your bank statements: regularly review your bank and credit card statements to identify recurring expenses and irregular spending. this can help you uncover subscriptions or services you no longer use.

4) identify emotional triggers: often, poor money habits are tied to emotions such as stress, boredom, or happiness. recognize situations that trigger impulsive spending or excessive splurging.

5) assess impulse purchases: take note of items you bought on a whim and rarely use. this indicates impulsive spending habits that can drain your finances.

6) evaluate debt levels: high levels of credit card debt, personal loans, or unpaid bills are clear signs of poor money management. these debts can accumulate quickly if not managed properly.

7) analyze savings patterns: review your savings history. are you consistently saving a portion of your income, or do you struggle to save at all? inadequate savings can indicate poor money habits.

8) consider financial goals: if you lack clear financial goals or a plan to achieve them, it's a sign of poor money habits. without goals, you might not have the motivation to make wise financial decisions.

9) review investment choices: if you're investing without proper research or making impulsive investment decisions, you might be falling victim to poor investment habits.

10) communication about finances: discuss money matters with family members or a partner. poor communication about finances can lead to misunderstandings and poor financial decisions.

11) avoiding budgeting: neglecting to create and stick to a budget can lead to overspending and not knowing where your money is going.

12) neglecting financial education: if you're not actively seeking knowledge about personal finance, you might be missing out on opportunities to improve your financial habits.

13) living beyond your means: continuously spending more than you earn can lead to debt and financial stress. recognize signs of living beyond your means, such as relying on credit cards to cover basic expenses.

14) failing to plan for the future: ignoring retirement planning, emergency funds, and insurance needs can leave you financially vulnerable in the long run.

15) reviewing long-term trends: look at your financial behavior over several months or years. are you consistently making the same poor money decisions?

once you've identified your poor money habits, it's time to take action:

1) set clear goals: define short-term and long-term financial goals to provide direction and motivation for improving your habits.

2) create a budget: develop a realistic budget that allocates funds to necessities, savings, and discretionary spending.

3) educate yourself: learn about personal finance, budgeting, investing, and debt management to make informed decisions.

4) practice self-control: before making a purchase, give yourself time to consider whether it aligns with your goals and needs, rather than giving in to impulses.

5) limit temptations: unsubscribe from shopping emails, avoid window shopping, and limit exposure to situations that trigger impulsive spending.

6) savings: set up automatic transfers to your savings and investment accounts to ensure consistent contributions.

7) review regularly: continuously monitor your progress, adjust your budget as needed, and celebrate achievements.

8) seek professional help: if your poor money habits are deeply ingrained or leading to significant financial distress, consider seeking help from a financial advisor or counselor.

remember, changing habits takes time and effort. be patient with yourself as you work towards improving your relationship with money.

CHAPTER TWO

SELF-REFLECTION AND AWARENESS

self-reflection and awareness are fundamental aspects of personal growth and development. they involve the ability to introspectively examine one's thoughts, emotions, behaviors, and experiences, leading to a deeper understanding of oneself. this process is a cornerstone of emotional intelligence and can have profound effects on various aspects of life, including relationships, decision-making, and overall well-being.

self-reflection involves taking the time to contemplate and analyze one's thoughts, actions, and experiences. it requires a certain level of mindfulness and willingness to confront both positive and negative aspects of oneself. through self-reflection, individuals can identify patterns of behavior, triggers for emotional responses, and underlying beliefs that shape their perceptions of the world.

awareness, on the other hand, encompasses the ability to be present in the moment and fully attuned to one's surroundings, emotions, and thoughts. it involves cultivating a state of mindfulness that allows individuals to observe their internal experiences without judgment. this heightened awareness enables individuals to respond to situations rather than react impulsively, fostering better control over their behavior and emotions.

both self-reflection and awareness are interconnected processes that feed into each other. self-reflection leads to increased self-awareness, as individuals begin to recognize their strengths, weaknesses, values, and aspirations. on the other hand, heightened awareness facilitates more effective self-reflection, as individuals become attuned to their inner experiences and are better equipped to analyze and understand them.

practicing self-reflection and awareness often involves various techniques, such as journaling, meditation, mindfulness exercises, and seeking feedback from trusted individuals. keeping a reflective journal allows individuals to document their thoughts and experiences over time, aiding in the identification of patterns and changes in behavior. meditation and mindfulness practices train the mind to focus on the present moment, enhancing awareness of one's thoughts and emotions as they arise.

benefits of cultivating self-reflection and awareness are multifaceted. they enable individuals to:

1) enhance emotional intelligence: by understanding their emotions and the underlying reasons behind them, individuals can develop better emotional regulation and empathy towards others.

2) improve decision-making: self-awareness helps individuals recognize their values and priorities, leading to more aligned and thoughtful decision-making.

3) strengthen relationships: understanding one's triggers and communication patterns can lead to healthier interactions and improved relationships.

4) personal growth: identifying areas for improvement and setting meaningful goals becomes easier when one is attuned to their strengths and weaknesses.

5) reduce stress: being present and aware of one's thoughts can reduce rumination about the past or anxiety about the future, leading to decreased stress levels.

6) enhance creativity: increased self-awareness can uncover hidden talents and perspectives, fostering creativity and innovation.

7) boost resilience: self-reflection allows individuals to understand how they have overcome challenges in the past, increasing their ability to cope with future difficulties.

8) authenticity: when individuals know themselves deeply, they can live more authentically by aligning their actions with their true selves.

it's important to note that self-reflection and awareness are ongoing processes that require patience and commitment. they involve confronting uncomfortable truths, acknowledging vulnerabilities, and being open to change. engaging in these practices can be challenging, but the rewards in terms of personal growth and well-being are significant. as individuals continue to delve into their inner selves, they can foster a greater sense of purpose, fulfillment, and a deeper connection with the world around them.

common financial pitfalls to watch out for
certainly! avoiding financial pitfalls is crucial for maintaining a healthy financial situation. here are some common financial pitfalls to watch out for:

1) living beyond your means: spending more than you earn can quickly lead to debt. it's important to create a budget, track your expenses, and prioritize needs over wants.

2) not having an emergency fund: without an emergency fund, unexpected expenses can lead to financial stress or even debt. aim to have 3-6 months' worth of living expenses set aside in a savings account.

3) high-interest debt: accumulating high-interest debt, such as credit card debt, can be financially draining. strive to pay off high-interest debts as quickly as possible to avoid excessive interest payments.

4) neglecting retirement savings: not saving for retirement early enough can lead to a shortfall in your golden years. start saving for retirement as soon as possible and take advantage of employer-sponsored plans like 401(k)s.

5) overlooking insurance needs: not having adequate insurance coverage, such as health, auto, home, or life insurance, cdecisionsan leave you vulnerable to significant financial setbacks in the event of accidents, illnesses, or disasters.

6) failing to invest wisely: not investing or making impulsive investment can hinder wealth-building opportunities. educate yourself about different investment options and consider seeking professional advice.

7) ignoring financial goals: lack of clear financial goals can lead to aimless spending and poor money management. set short-term and long-term financial goals to stay focused on your priorities.

8) not reviewing financial statements: neglecting to review bank statements, credit card bills, and other financial statements can lead to missed errors, fraudulent activities, or oversights.

9) impulse buying: giving in to impulsive purchases without considering their impact on your budget can quickly add up and strain your finances.

10) not negotiating: whether it's your salary, bills, or contracts, failing to negotiate can lead to missed opportunities for saving or earning more money.

11) co-signing loans: co-signing a loan for someone else can put your credit and finances at risk if the borrower defaults. be cautious before co-signing and understand the potential consequences.

12) ignoring interest rates: ignoring fluctuating interest rates on loans or mortgages can result in missed chances to refinance and save money over the long term.

13) relying solely on credit: depending solely on credit cards for purchases can lead to overspending and accumulating debt. use credit responsibly and within your means.

14) not diversifying investments: putting all your investments in one asset or industry can expose you to higher risks. diversify your investment portfolio to mitigate potential losses.

15) underestimating small expenses: small, recurring expenses can add up over time. keep track of subscriptions, memberships, and other recurring costs to avoid overspending.

avoiding these financial pitfalls requires awareness, discipline, and proactive decision-making. regularly reviewing your financial situation and seeking guidance from financial professionals can help you stay on track towards achieving your financial goals.

THE PATH TO FINANCIAL FREEDOM

the path to financial freedom is a journey that involves careful planning, disciplined habits, and a solid understanding of personal finance. it's the process of attaining a level of financial stability where you have the means to support your desired lifestyle without constantly worrying about money. this journey can be broken down into several key components:

1) financial education: the first step is to educate yourself about basic financial concepts. this includes understanding budgeting, saving, investing, debt management, and various investment vehicles. taking the time to learn about these topics will empower you to make informed decisions about your money.

2) setting clear goals: financial freedom is different for everyone. it might involve paying off debts, saving for a comfortable retirement, buying a home, or funding a passion project. setting clear and achievable financial goals is crucial, as these goals will guide your decisions and keep you motivated.

3) creating a budget: a budget is the foundation of financial planning. it helps you track your income, expenses, and savings. creating a budget allows you to allocate your money efficiently, cut unnecessary spending, and ensure you're living within your means.

4) saving and investing: saving a portion of your income is essential for building an emergency fund and meeting short-term goals. however, achieving financial freedom often requires investing to grow your wealth over time. diversified investments, such as stocks, bonds, real estate, and mutual funds, can help your money work for you.

5) debt management: paying off high-interest debt should be a priority. high-interest debts can accumulate quickly and hinder your progress toward financial freedom. once you've cleared high-interest debts, you can focus on managing and leveraging low-interest debts, like a mortgage.

6) living below your means: consistently spending less than you earn is a key principle of financial freedom. it allows you to save and invest more, which accelerates your journey towards your financial goals.

7) passive income streams: building passive income streams, such as rental income, dividends, or royalties, can provide a consistent cash flow without requiring constant effort. passive income can significantly contribute to your financial stability and freedom.

8) continued learning and adaptation: the world of finance is dynamic. staying updated with financial trends, economic shifts, and new investment opportunities is crucial. adapt your strategies as needed to align with changing circumstances.

9) patience and discipline: achieving financial freedom is a marathon, not a sprint. it requires patience and discipline to stay on track, especially during challenging times or periods of market volatility.

10) estate planning: as you accumulate wealth, it's important to plan for the future by creating a will, setting up trusts, and making arrangements

for the orderly transfer of your assets. estate planning ensures that your financial legacy is managed according to your wishes.

remember that the path to financial freedom is not a linear process. it involves making adjustments, learning from mistakes, and staying committed to your goals. every individual's journey is unique, influenced by personal circumstances, risk tolerance, and aspirations. the key is to start early, stay consistent, and keep your long-term vision in mind.

CHAPTER THREE

SETTING CLEAR FINANCIAL GOALS

setting clear financial goals is a crucial step towards achieving financial success and securing your future. without well-defined goals, it's easy to drift aimlessly through life, making impulsive decisions that might not align with your long-term aspirations. whether your goals involve buying a home, saving for retirement, paying off debt, or going on a dream vacation, having a structured plan in place can make a significant difference.

1) define your goals: start by identifying your financial aspirations. these could be short-term goals like paying off credit card debt, medium-term goals like saving for a down payment on a house, or long-term goals like building a retirement fund. each goal should be specific, measurable, achievable, relevant, and time-bound (smart).

2) quantify your goals: assign a monetary value to each goal. this provides clarity and allows you to determine how much you need to save or invest to reach your target. for instance, if you're planning to buy a house, calculate the down payment and associated costs.

3) prioritize: not all goals are equally important. prioritize them based on their significance and urgency. it might be helpful to categorize goals as essential (e.g., building an emergency fund), important (e.g., saving for a child's education), and aspirational (e.g., luxury travel).

4) break down goals: divide big goals into smaller, manageable steps. this makes the process less daunting and helps you track your progress. for instance, if you're aiming to save $50,000 for a down payment, break it into monthly or yearly saving targets.

5) set timeframes: assign deadlines to your goals. having a timeframe creates a sense of urgency and prevents procrastination. it also helps in planning and allocating resources efficiently.

6) consider financial constraints: evaluate your current financial situation and identify potential constraints. this might involve analyzing your income, expenses, and debt. realistic goal-setting considers your financial limitations while still pushing you to achieve more.

7) research and plan: research the steps required to achieve your goals. if you're investing, learn about different investment options. if you're saving for education, understand the costs and potential funding sources. a well-informed plan is more likely to succeed.

8) monitor and adjust: regularly review your progress. if you're falling behind, reassess your strategy. life circumstances can change, and your goals might need adjustment. be flexible while staying focused on the end result.

9) celebrate milestones: recognize and celebrate your achievements along the way. this boosts motivation and makes the journey towards your larger goal more enjoyable.

10) seek professional advice: depending on your goals, it might be beneficial to consult financial advisors, tax professionals, or investment experts. they can provide tailored advice based on your unique situation.

11) accountability: share your goals with a trusted friend or family member who can hold you accountable. this external encouragement can help you stay on track, especially during challenging times.

12) visualize your success: imagine how your life will improve once you achieve your financial goals. visualization can inspire you to remain disciplined and dedicated to your plan.

in conclusion, setting clear financial goals is a cornerstone of effective financial management. it provides direction, purpose, and a roadmap for your financial journey. by following these steps and staying committed, you can work towards achieving your aspirations and securing your financial future.

BUILDING A STRONG FOUNDATION FOR BETTER HABITS

building a strong foundation for better habits is essential for personal growth and positive transformation. habits play a crucial role in shaping our behaviors and ultimately determining our success and well-being. here's an extensive guide on how to establish a solid foundation for cultivating better habits:

1) self-awareness: begin by identifying the habits you currently have and understanding their impact on your life. reflect on both positive and negative habits, as well as the triggers that lead to them. this self-awareness forms the basis for change.

2) clear goals: define what you want to achieve through new habits. whether it's improved health, increased productivity, or enhanced relationships, having clear goals provides direction and motivation.

3) start small: begin with one or two habits that are manageable and achievable. starting small prevents overwhelm and increases the likelihood of success. once these habits become ingrained, you can gradually add more.

4) consistency: consistency is key to habit formation. commit to performing the desired behavior daily or at a set frequency. consistency reinforces the neural pathways associated with the habit, making it more automatic over time.

5) create triggers: associate your new habit with an existing cue or trigger. for example, if you want to develop a habit of stretching in the morning, do it right after brushing your teeth. this linkage makes the habit easier to remember and execute.

6) accountability: share your goals with a friend, family member, or mentor who can hold you accountable. reporting your progress to someone else increases your commitment to sticking with the habit.

7) positive environment: surround yourself with an environment that supports your desired habits. for instance, if you're trying to eat healthier, stock your kitchen with nutritious foods and remove unhealthy snacks.

8) use rewards: reward yourself for successfully practicing the habit. positive reinforcement strengthens the habit loop in your brain. however, ensure the rewards align with your overall goal – for example, don't reward yourself with junk food if you're trying to eat better.

9) mindfulness and reflection: practice mindfulness to become more aware of your actions and thoughts. regularly reflect on your progress, challenges, and adjustments needed. this self-reflection helps you stay on track and adapt your approach as necessary.

10) overcoming setbacks: setbacks are natural when building habits. instead of getting discouraged, view them as learning opportunities. analyze what led to the setback and strategize how to prevent it in the future.

11) tracking and measurement: keep a record of your habit-related activities. use a journal, app, or calendar to track your progress. monitoring your consistency and incremental improvements can be motivating.

12) education and skill-building: equip yourself with the knowledge and skills needed for the habit. if you're trying to incorporate regular exercise, for instance, learn about proper techniques and safe practices.

13) flexibility: be willing to adjust your approach if a habit isn't working as planned. flexibility doesn't mean giving up; it means finding alternative methods that suit your personality and circumstances better.

14) patience: habits take time to develop. research suggests that it takes around 66 days on average for a behavior to become a habit. be patient and persistent in your efforts.

15) celebrate progress: acknowledge and celebrate your achievements along the way. small victories contribute to your overall sense of accomplishment and motivate you to continue building better habits.

remember, building a strong foundation for better habits is a continuous journey. the process requires dedication, self-compassion, and a willingness to learn and adapt. over time, the habits you cultivate will become an integral part of your lifestyle, contributing to your personal and professional growth.

Breaking Bad Habits

breaking bad habits can be a challenging yet immensely rewarding endeavor. habits are deeply ingrained patterns of behavior that we often engage in without conscious thought. whether it's biting your nails, overeating, procrastinating, or smoking, bad habits can have detrimental effects on our physical, mental, and emotional well-being. here's a comprehensive guide on how to effectively break free from these patterns:

1) self-awareness: the first step is recognizing the habit you want to change. be honest with yourself about why you engage in it, the triggers that prompt it, and the consequences it brings. this self-awareness lays the foundation for change.

2) set clear intentions: clearly define your reasons for wanting to break the habit. whether it's improving your health, boosting productivity, or

enhancing your relationships, having a strong motivation will fuel your determination.

3) small: trying to completely eliminate a habit overnight can be overwhelming. begin with small, manageable changes. for instance, if you're trying to cut down on sugar intake, start by reducing the amount of sugar in your coffee.

4) replace with positive behavior: habits often fill a void or meet a need. replace the negative habit with a positive behavior that fulfills the same need. if you're trying to quit mindless snacking, replace it with a healthier snack or a short walk.

5) identify triggers: pinpoint the situations, emotions, or environments that trigger the habit. this awareness allows you to develop strategies to avoid or cope with these triggers effectively.

6) create a support system: share your goal with friends, family, or a support group. having people who encourage and hold you accountable can significantly increase your chances of success.

7) use positive reinforcement: reward yourself for each milestone achieved. this could be treating yourself to something enjoyable, as it helps associate breaking the habit with positive outcomes.

8) practice mindfulness: mindfulness techniques can help you become more conscious of your actions and impulses. this awareness enables you to pause and make a conscious choice instead of falling into automatic behaviors.

9) visualize success: visualize yourself successfully breaking the habit. this mental imagery enhances your belief in your ability to change and reinforces your commitment.

10) learn from relapses: it's common to experience setbacks along the way. instead of viewing relapses as failures, treat them as learning opportunities. analyze what triggered the relapse and develop strategies to handle similar situations better in the future.

11) persistence is key: breaking a habit takes time and effort. stay patient and persistent. remember that change is a process, and setbacks don't define your journey.

12) seek professional help: for deeply ingrained or addictive habits, seeking help from a therapist, counselor, or support group can provide valuable guidance and strategies.

13) modify your environment: make changes in your surroundings to reduce the temptation to engage in the habit. for instance, if you're trying to reduce screen time, keep devices out of sight during designated periods.

14) track your progress: keep a journal or use habit-tracking apps to monitor your progress. this helps you stay accountable and see how far you've come.

15) celebrate milestones: celebrate your achievements at various stages. breaking a habit is a significant accomplishment, and acknowledging your progress boosts your self-confidence.

remember that breaking bad habits is a journey that requires commitment, self-compassion, and resilience. it's about making consistent choices that align with your desired outcomes. with time, effort, and the right strategies, you can successfully overcome even the most entrenched habits.

chapter four
STRATEGIES FOR OVERCOMING IMPULSE SPENDING

impulse spending, also known as impulsive buying or emotional buying, refers to the act of making unplanned purchases on a whim without considering the long-term consequences. this behavior can have a negative impact on personal finances and overall financial well-being. to overcome impulse spending, consider implementing the following strategies:

1) create a budget: establish a clear and realistic budget that outlines your monthly income, expenses, and savings goals. knowing exactly how much you can spend on discretionary items can help you make informed decisions and curb impulse buying.

2) identify triggers: recognize the situations, emotions, or environments that trigger your impulse spending. whether it's stress, boredom, peer pressure, or retail displays, understanding your triggers can help you avoid or manage them effectively.

3) practice mindful shopping: before making a purchase, take a moment to pause and ask yourself whether you truly need the item. consider whether it aligns with your budget, values, and long-term goals. mindful shopping encourages intentional decision-making.

4) implement a waiting period: implement a waiting period before making non-essential purchases. for example, give yourself 24 hours or a week to reconsider the purchase. this delay can help you evaluate whether the item is a genuine need or just a passing desire.

5) use shopping lists: prepare a detailed shopping list before heading to the store or shopping online. stick to the list and avoid deviating from it, even if you come across tempting deals or items.

6) avoid impulse environments: limit exposure to environments that encourage impulsive spending, such as malls or online shopping platforms. unsubscribe from promotional emails and unfollow social media accounts that frequently showcase products.

7) set financial goals: establish short-term and long-term financial goals, such as saving for a vacation, buying a home, or paying off debt. focusing on these goals can motivate you to prioritize saving over impulsive purchases.

8) use cash or debit cards: leave credit cards at home when you go shopping, and opt for cash or a debit card instead. physical payment

methods make the spending process more tangible, helping you become more conscious of your purchases.

9) practice self-care: find healthy and constructive ways to manage emotions like stress, anxiety, or boredom. engage in activities you enjoy, exercise, meditate, or spend time with loved ones to reduce the urge to shop impulsively.

10) unsubscribe and unfollow: clear your inbox of retail emails and unfollow brands on social media that consistently tempt you with offers and promotions. less exposure to such marketing can reduce the temptation to spend impulsively.

11) compare prices: before purchasing, take time to research and compare prices across different stores or online platforms. this not only helps you find the best deal but also gives you time to reconsider the purchase.

12) track your spending: keep a record of all your expenses, including small purchases. reviewing your spending patterns can highlight areas where impulse spending is occurring and help you make necessary adjustments.

remember that overcoming impulse spending is a gradual process that requires self-awareness and discipline. implementing these strategies consistently can help you regain control over your spending habits and work toward a more financially secure future.

MANAGING PROCRASTINATION AND AVOIDANCE

managing procrastination and avoidance is crucial for maintaining productivity and achieving one's goals. procrastination refers to the act of delaying tasks that need to be completed, often opting for short-term pleasure or comfort instead. avoidance, on the other hand, involves intentionally evading tasks that may trigger discomfort, anxiety, or stress. both tendencies can hinder personal and professional growth, but there are several strategies to effectively manage them:

1) self-awareness: recognizing when you're procrastinating or avoiding tasks is the first step. reflect on your behaviors and thoughts to identify patterns and triggers. this awareness will help you intervene early and implement strategies to overcome these tendencies.

2) break tasks into smaller steps: large tasks can feel overwhelming and lead to avoidance. break them into smaller, manageable steps. completing these smaller portions can provide a sense of accomplishment and motivate you to continue working.

3) set clear goals: define specific, measurable, achievable, relevant, and time-bound (smart) goals. clarity about what needs to be achieved and by when can reduce the tendency to procrastinate.

4) use time management techniques: techniques like the pomodoro technique (working for a focused 25-minute period followed by a 5-minute break) can enhance concentration and reduce the likelihood of procrastination.

5) prioritize tasks: arrange tasks in order of importance. tackling high-priority tasks first can reduce the inclination to procrastinate on less important tasks.

6) create a routine: establishing a daily routine can help eliminate decision fatigue and create a structured environment that minimizes opportunities for avoidance.

7) minimize distractions: identify and minimize sources of distraction, such as social media, emails, or noisy environments. this can help you maintain focus on the task at hand.

8) reward system: create a rewards system for completing tasks on time. treat yourself to something enjoyable after completing a task, reinforcing positive behavior.

9) mindfulness and self-compassion: practicing mindfulness can help you become more aware of your thoughts and emotions, reducing the

likelihood of avoidance. self-compassion can counteract negative self-talk and promote a more forgiving attitude toward setbacks.

10) visualize success and consequences: imagine the positive outcomes of completing a task and the negative consequences of avoiding it. this mental exercise can motivate you to take action.

11) accountability: share your goals with a friend, family member, or colleague who can hold you accountable. knowing that someone is tracking your progress can discourage procrastination.

12) manage perfectionism: perfectionism can lead to avoidance due to fear of failure. shift your focus from perfection to progress and learning. accept that mistakes are a natural part of growth.

13) limit planning: while planning is essential, excessive planning can become a form of procrastination itself. set a time limit for planning and commit to taking action afterward.

14) understand resistance: explore the reasons behind your resistance to certain tasks. identifying underlying fears or negative beliefs can help you address them directly.

15) seek professional help: if procrastination or avoidance significantly impairs your daily life or mental well-being, consider seeking support from a therapist or counselor who specializes in cognitive-behavioral techniques.

remember that overcoming procrastination and avoidance is a gradual process that requires consistent effort. implementing these strategies and adapting them to your personal preferences can help you become more productive, achieve your goals, and lead a more fulfilling life.

CULTIVATING HEALTHY MONEY HABITS

cultivating healthy money habits is essential for achieving financial stability and long-term success. these habits are the building blocks of sound financial management and can have a profound impact on your overall well-being. here are some key steps and practices to consider:

1) budgeting: start by creating a budget that outlines your monthly income and expenses. this will help you track where your money is going and identify areas where you can cut back or save.

2) tracking expenses: keep a record of every expense, no matter how small. this will give you a clear picture of your spending patterns and help you make informed decisions about where to allocate your funds.

3) living within your means: avoid overspending and try to live within your means. this means not relying heavily on credit cards or loans to finance your lifestyle.

4) emergency fund: build an emergency fund that covers three to six months' worth of living expenses. this will provide a safety net in case of unexpected events like medical emergencies or job loss.

5) saving regularly: develop a habit of saving a portion of your income regularly. consider setting up automatic transfers to a savings account to make this process easier.

6) setting financial goals: define both short-term and long-term financial goals. these could include paying off debt, buying a home, saving for retirement, or taking a dream vacation.

7) debt management: prioritize paying off high-interest debts like credit card balances. create a plan to tackle your debts systematically while still maintaining your other financial obligations.

8) wisely: educate yourself about different investment options and consider seeking professional advice. investing can help your money grow over time and work towards your long-term goals.

9) delayed gratification: practice delayed gratification by distinguishing between needs and wants. before making a purchase, give yourself time to think if it aligns with your financial goals.

10) avoid impulse buying: impulse purchases can derail your budget. make a habit of waiting a day or two before making non-essential purchases to ensure you genuinely need or want the item.

11) regular review: periodically review your financial situation, including your budget, savings, investments, and debts. adjust your plans as necessary to stay on track.

12) continuous learning: stay informed about personal finance topics. read books, articles, and attend workshops to enhance your financial literacy and decision-making skills.

13) avoid comparison: everyone's financial journey is different. avoid comparing your progress to others, as this can lead to unnecessary stress and poor financial decisions.

14) negotiate and shop smart: negotiate for better deals, and shop around for discounts or better prices before making significant purchases.

15) mindful spending: practice mindful spending by considering the value a purchase adds to your life. focus on experiences and items that genuinely contribute to your well-being and happiness.

16) regularly review financial goals: revisit your financial goals and adjust them as needed based on changes in your life circumstances, income, and priorities.

remember, cultivating healthy money habits is a gradual process that requires discipline and consistency. by implementing these practices, you can create a strong foundation for financial success and reduce stress related to money management.

CHAPTER FIVE

BUDGETING AND TRACKING YOUR EXPENSE

budgeting and tracking expenses are essential financial practices that help individuals and households manage their money effectively. these practices provide a clear overview of income, spending habits, and financial goals, enabling better decision-making and ensuring financial stability. let's delve into the details of budgeting and expense tracking:

budgeting:
budgeting involves creating a plan for how you will allocate your income across various categories such as housing, transportation, groceries, entertainment, savings, and more. the primary goal of budgeting is to ensure that your expenses do not exceed your income, allowing you to achieve your financial objectives. here's how to create an effective budget:

1) calculate income: start by determining your total monthly income, including salaries, bonuses, side gigs, and any other sources of revenue.

2) identify fixed expenses: list your fixed expenses, such as rent/mortgage, utilities, insurance, and loan payments. these are consistent amounts that need to be paid regularly.

3) list variable expenses: identify variable expenses like groceries, dining out, entertainment, and discretionary spending. these expenses can fluctuate month to month.

4) set financial goals: define short-term and long-term financial goals, such as building an emergency fund, saving for a vacation, or paying off debt. allocate funds towards these goals in your budget.

5) allocate categories: divide your income into categories based on your expenses. assign limits to each category, ensuring that your total expenses are lower than your income.

6) track progress: regularly review your budget to track your progress. adjust your allocations as needed to stay on track and accommodate changes in your financial situation.

expense tracking:
expense tracking involves monitoring and recording every expense you
make. this practice helps you understand your spending patterns,
identify areas where you can cut back, and stay accountable to your
budget. here's how to effectively track your expenses:

1) choose tracking method: decide whether you want to track expenses
manually using a notebook or spreadsheet or use digital tools and apps
for automated tracking.

2) categorize expenses: categorize your expenses into groups like
groceries, utilities, transportation, entertainment, and more. this will
help you analyze your spending patterns.

3) every expense: consistently record every expense, no matter how
small. this includes cash purchases, credit/debit card transactions, and
online payments.

4) review regularly: set a specific time each week or month to review
your tracked expenses. compare your spending against your budget to
see if you're staying on track.

5) analyze trends: look for patterns and trends in your spending. are
there categories where you consistently overspend? identifying these
areas will help you make adjustments.

6) adjust your budget: based on the insights gained from expense
tracking, adjust your budget as necessary. you might need to reallocate
funds or make conscious efforts to reduce spending in certain areas.

7) stay disciplined: expense tracking requires discipline and consistency.
stay committed to recording every expense to get an accurate picture of
your financial situation.

in summary, budgeting and tracking expenses are powerful tools that
promote financial awareness and discipline. by creating a well-structured
budget and diligently tracking your spending, you can work towards

achieving your financial goals, minimizing debt, and building a more secure financial future.

SAVING AND INVESTING WISELY

certainly! saving and investing wisely are crucial components of financial planning that can help individuals achieve their long-term financial goals, build wealth, and secure their future. let's delve into each of these aspects in detail.

saving wisely:

saving involves setting aside a portion of your income for future needs and unexpected expenses. here are some key principles for saving wisely:

1) set clear goals: determine your financial objectives, such as creating an emergency fund, saving for a home, education, retirement, or other specific goals.

2) budgeting: create a budget to track your income and expenses. this helps identify areas where you can cut back and allocate more funds toward savings.

3) fund: build an emergency fund that covers 3 to 6 months' worth of living expenses. this fund acts as a safety net during unexpected events like medical emergencies or job loss.

4) automate savings: set up automatic transfers to a separate savings account. this ensures a consistent saving habit and prevents you from spending money before saving.

5) debt management: prioritize paying off high-interest debts to save on interest payments. this frees up more money that can be directed towards savings.

investing wisely:

investing involves putting your money into assets with the potential to grow over time. here are important considerations for investing wisely:

1) understand risk and return: all investments carry some level of risk. higher potential returns often come with higher risk. assess your risk tolerance and invest accordingly.

2) diversification: spread your investments across different asset classes (stocks, bonds, real estate, etc.) to reduce risk. diversification helps mitigate losses if one investment underperforms.

3) time horizon: consider your investment timeline. short-term goals may warrant more conservative investments, while long-term goals can tolerate more risk for potentially higher returns.

4) research and education: thoroughly research investments before committing funds. understand the market trends, historical performance, and the company's financial health if you're investing in stocks.

5) costs and fees: be aware of investment fees, such as management fees for mutual funds or transaction fees for buying/selling stocks. high fees can eat into your returns over time.

6) avoid emotional decision-making: market fluctuations are natural. avoid making impulsive decisions based on short-term market movements. stick to your long-term investment strategy.

7) regular review: periodically review your investment portfolio to ensure it aligns with your goals and risk tolerance. rebalancing may be necessary to maintain your desired asset allocation.

8) professional advice: consider seeking advice from financial advisors or investment professionals. they can provide personalized guidance based on your financial situation and goals.

remember that saving and investing wisely are ongoing processes. adjustments may be needed as your life circumstances change.

continuously educate yourself about financial matters to make informed decisions. both saving and investing require discipline, patience, and a long-term perspective to reap the benefits of compounding growth over time.

NAVIGATING CREDIT AND DEBT

navigating credit and debt is a crucial aspect of personal finance management. it involves understanding how credit works, using it wisely, and managing debt responsibly to maintain financial health and avoid potential pitfalls. here's an in-depth exploration of the topic:

understanding credit:
credit refers to the ability to borrow money with the promise of repayment in the future. it enables individuals to make purchases, invest, or handle emergencies without having to pay upfront. credit is typically extended in various forms, including credit cards, loans, and lines of credit. to navigate credit effectively, it's important to understand key concepts:

1) credit score: your credit score, often represented as a three-digit number, reflects your creditworthiness. it's based on factors such as payment history, credit utilization, length of credit history, types of credit, and recent credit inquiries.

2) credit report: this is a detailed record of your credit history, including accounts, payment history, and any negative items. regularly reviewing your credit report helps you identify errors and maintain accurate information.

3) credit utilization: this is the ratio of your credit card balances to your credit limits. keeping this ratio low (typically below 30%) demonstrates responsible credit use and can positively impact your credit score.

using credit wisely:
to navigate credit successfully, consider the following tips:

1) create a budget: establish a budget to track your income and expenses. this helps you allocate funds for credit payments and prevents overspending.

2) pay on time: timely payments are crucial for maintaining a good credit score. late payments can lead to increased interest rates and negative impacts on your credit history.

3) avoid overspending: just because you have available credit doesn't mean you should use it all. only borrow what you can comfortably repay to avoid accumulating unnecessary debt.

4) diversify credit: having a mix of credit types (e.g., credit cards, installment loans) can positively affect your credit score, as it shows your ability to manage different types of credit.

managing debt:
debt management involves handling existing debts effectively to avoid financial strain and ensure long-term financial well-being:

1) prioritize high-interest debt: pay off high-interest debts, such as credit card balances, first. the interest on these debts can accumulate quickly and hinder your ability to pay down the principal.

2) debt snowball vs. debt avalanche: two popular debt repayment strategies are the snowball method (paying off smallest debts first) and the avalanche method (paying off highest-interest debts first). choose the approach that suits your financial situation and psychology.

3) consolidation and refinancing: in some cases, consolidating multiple debts into a single loan or refinancing existing loans can lower interest rates and simplify payments.

4) emergency fund: building an emergency fund can help prevent relying on credit during unexpected financial challenges, reducing the risk of accruing more debt.

5) seek professional help: if you're struggling with debt, consider consulting a credit counselor or financial advisor. they can provide guidance tailored to your situation.

avoiding debt traps:
to navigate credit and debt successfully, be aware of potential pitfalls:

1) predatory lending: be cautious of lenders offering high-interest loans or credit cards with hidden fees. read terms carefully before committing.

2) minimum payments: making only minimum payments on credit cards can lead to a cycle of debt, as most of your payment goes towards interest rather than reducing the principal.

3) using credit for non-essentials: avoid using credit for discretionary purchases that you can't afford to pay off in the near term.

4) ignoring warning signs: if you're consistently struggling to make payments, it's important to address the issue proactively rather than letting it escalate.

in conclusion, navigating credit and debt involves understanding credit concepts, using credit wisely, managing debt effectively, and avoiding common traps. responsible credit use and prudent debt management are crucial for achieving financial stability and long-term success. regularly educating yourself about personal finance and seeking professional advice when needed can contribute to your overall financial well-being.

CHAPTER SIX

UNDERSTANDING CREDIT SCORES AND REPORTS

understanding credit scores and reports is crucial for managing your financial health and making informed decisions about credit-related matters. credit scores are numerical representations of an individual's creditworthiness, indicating how likely they are to repay borrowed money. credit reports, on the other hand, are detailed records of a person's credit history and financial behavior. let's delve into these concepts more deeply:

credit scores:

1) calculation: credit scores are typically calculated using a mathematical formula that evaluates various aspects of your credit history. commonly used scoring models include fico (fair isaac corporation) score and vantagescore. factors like payment history, credit utilization, length of credit history, types of credit, and recent credit inquiries influence these scores.

2) range and interpretation: fico scores range from 300 to 850, with higher scores indicating better creditworthiness. generally, scores above 700 are considered good, while those above 800 are excellent. lower scores might result in difficulties obtaining loans or credit at favorable terms.

3) influencing factors: payment history (whether you've paid your bills on time), credit utilization (how much of your available credit you're using), length of credit history, types of credit (credit cards, mortgages, etc.), and recent credit inquiries impact your score. a history of late payments or high credit card balances can lower your score.

4) importance: credit scores are used by lenders to assess your risk as a borrower. they play a significant role in determining whether you qualify for credit, the interest rates you'll receive, and the credit limits you'll be granted.

credit reports:

1) credit reports are compiled by credit bureaus (equifax, experian, and transunion) based on data provided by creditors, lenders, and public records. they contain detailed information about your credit history, including credit accounts, payment history, balances, and more.

2) sections: credit reports consist of sections such as personal information (name, address, etc.), credit accounts (credit cards, loans,

mortgages), payment history (on-time and late payments), credit inquiries (requests for your credit report), and public records (bankruptcies, tax liens).

3) regular review: it's advisable to review your credit reports regularly to identify errors, inaccuracies, or fraudulent activity. under the fair credit reporting act (fcra), you're entitled to a free credit report from each bureau annually, which you can request from annualcreditreport.com.

4) disputes and corrections: if you find errors in your credit report, you can dispute them with the credit bureau. they are required to investigate and correct inaccuracies. this process can help improve your credit score if errors are resolved.

in essence, understanding credit scores and reports empowers you to manage your finances effectively. by maintaining a good credit history, you can qualify for better loan terms, lower interest rates, and access to various financial opportunities. regular monitoring of your credit reports ensures the accuracy of the information being used to calculate your credit score. this, in turn, enables you to take steps to improve your credit standing and achieve your financial goals.

TACKLING DEBT AND AVOIDING HIGH-INTEREST TRAPS

tackling debt and avoiding high-interest traps are essential financial skills that can have a profound impact on one's financial well-being. whether you're dealing with existing debt or striving to prevent future debt, here are some strategies to consider:

tackling debt:

1) assessment and prioritization: start by gathering all your debt information, including balances, interest rates, and minimum payments. categorize your debts as high-interest (credit cards, payday loans) or low-interest (mortgage, student loans). prioritize paying off high-interest debts first.

2) create a budget: develop a comprehensive budget that outlines your income and expenses. this will help you identify areas where you can cut back on spending and allocate more funds toward debt repayment.

debt repayment strategies:

1) snowball method: pay the minimum on all debts except the smallest one. put extra money towards the smallest debt until it's paid off, then move to the next smallest. this method offers psychological motivation as you see debts being cleared.
2) avalanche method: prioritize paying off the debt with the highest interest rate first. this saves you the most money in the long run by reducing overall interest payments.
3) debt consolidation: consider consolidating high-interest debts into a single, lower-interest loan. this can make repayments more manageable and save you money on interest.
4) negotiate with creditors: if you're struggling to make payments, contact your creditors to discuss options. they might be willing to negotiate a lower interest rate or a more manageable repayment plan.

5) side hustles and extra income: explore opportunities to increase your income through part-time jobs, freelancing, or selling items you no longer need. the extra funds can be directed towards debt repayment.

avoiding high-interest traps:

1) emergency fund: build an emergency fund to cover unexpected expenses. having this safety net can prevent you from resorting to high-interest loans or credit cards in times of crisis.

2) smart credit card use: credit cards can be convenient, but they often come with high-interest rates. pay your credit card balance in full each month to avoid accruing interest. if you carry a balance, look for cards with lower interest rates.

3) research and compare: before taking on any form of debt, research different options and compare interest rates and terms. this applies to loans, credit cards, and any financial products you're considering.

4) avoid payday loans: these short-term, high-interest loans can quickly trap you in a cycle of debt. explore alternatives such as borrowing from family or friends, negotiating with creditors, or seeking assistance from non-profit credit counseling agencies.

5) educate yourself: understand how interest works, how different types of loans function, and the implications of missing payments. financial literacy is a powerful tool in avoiding high-interest debt traps.

6) live within your means: avoid the temptation to overspend or live a lifestyle beyond your financial means. practice disciplined spending and prioritize saving over unnecessary expenses.

7) invest in yourself: consider investing in education or skills that can increase your earning potential. this can help you avoid financial struggles in the long run.

tackling debt and avoiding high-interest traps require discipline, careful planning, and a willingness to make necessary lifestyle changes. by implementing these strategies, you can regain control of your finances and work towards a more secure and debt-free future.

BUILDING A SUPPORTIVE FINANCIAL ENVIRONMENT

building a supportive financial environment involves creating conditions that promote financial stability, growth, and well-being for individuals, families, businesses, and communities. this encompasses a range of factors, from government policies and regulations to personal financial education and cultural attitudes towards money. here's an in-depth exploration of the key components and strategies to achieve a supportive financial environment:

1) policy and regulation:
government policies play a crucial role in shaping the financial landscape. regulations that ensure consumer protection, fair lending practices, and financial transparency are essential. for example,

enforcing regulations that prevent predatory lending or fraudulent financial schemes helps create a safer environment for financial transactions.

2) access to financial services:
a supportive financial environment ensures that individuals and businesses have access to a range of financial services, including banking, credit, insurance, and investment opportunities. efforts to promote financial inclusion, especially among marginalized communities, can lead to improved economic outcomes.

3) financial literacy and education:
educating individuals about personal finance and money management is pivotal. schools, workplaces, and community organizations can offer financial literacy programs to teach skills like budgeting, saving, investing, and debt management. this empowers people to make informed financial decisions.

4) savings and investment incentives:
governments and institutions can provide incentives to encourage saving and investing. tax benefits for retirement contributions, matching funds for savings, and grants for business investments can motivate people to secure their financial futures.

5) support for entrepreneurs and small businesses:
a favorable environment for entrepreneurs and small businesses is essential for economic growth. access to affordable loans, business development resources, and mentorship programs can help these ventures thrive.

6) consumer protection and financial stability:
financial crises can have far-reaching impacts. regulatory measures and institutions that ensure the stability of financial markets, protect consumers from unfair practices, and regulate systemic risks are critical for maintaining a supportive environment.

7) cultural attitudes towards money:

societal attitudes towards money influence financial behaviors. encouraging a culture of responsible spending, saving, and investment can foster a healthier financial environment. this can involve changing perceptions about debt, savings, and long-term planning.

8) technological innovation:
technological advancements have transformed financial services. fintech solutions like mobile banking, digital wallets, and investment apps have increased access and convenience. embracing innovation can enhance financial inclusion and efficiency.

9) supportive workplace policies:
employers can contribute to a supportive financial environment by offering benefits like retirement plans, financial counseling, and flexible savings accounts. these initiatives help employees manage their finances effectively.

10) social safety nets:
comprehensive social safety nets, including unemployment benefits, healthcare coverage, and housing assistance, provide a safety net during difficult financial times, reducing the likelihood of individuals falling into severe financial distress.

11) collaboration and partnerships:
building a supportive financial environment requires collaboration among governments, financial institutions, educational institutions, nonprofits, and businesses. partnerships can leverage diverse expertise to create comprehensive strategies.

12) long-term vision and adaptability:
a sustainable financial environment requires a long-term perspective and adaptability to changing economic conditions. continuously evaluating policies and strategies and making necessary adjustments is crucial for ongoing success.

in summary, building a supportive financial environment involves a multifaceted approach that addresses policy, education, access, culture, and innovation. by prioritizing financial education, responsible lending practices, and inclusive policies, societies can work toward creating an environment where financial stability and prosperity are attainable for all.

CHAPTER SEVEN

COMMUNICATING WITH FAMILY AND FRIENDS ABOUT MONEY

communicating about money with family and friends is a vital aspect of maintaining healthy relationships and managing financial matters effectively. open and transparent discussions can help prevent misunderstandings, reduce conflicts, and ensure everyone involved is on the same page. here are some key points to consider when communicating about money:

1) choose the right time and place: select a neutral and comfortable environment for discussions about money. avoid bringing up financial topics during stressful moments or when emotions are running high.

2) be honest and open: honesty is crucial when discussing money matters. share your financial situation, goals, and concerns openly. transparency fosters trust and encourages others to reciprocate.

3) set clear boundaries: clearly define what topics are open for discussion and what should remain private. this prevents overstepping boundaries and maintains a respectful atmosphere.

4) active listening: pay attention to what others are saying without interruption. listen to their perspectives, needs, and concerns before expressing your own opinions.

5) avoid judgment: when discussing money, it's important to refrain from being judgmental or critical. people have different financial situations and goals, and empathy goes a long way in maintaining strong relationships.

6) discuss shared goals: if you have shared financial goals, such as planning a vacation or buying a property together, discuss them openly. this helps align everyone's efforts and ensures everyone is committed to the same objectives.

7) respect differences: understand that people have different financial priorities and beliefs. what may seem important to you might not hold the same significance for others. respect these differences to avoid conflicts.

8) be patient: financial conversations can be complex and emotional. be patient, especially if the topic is sensitive. give others time to process information and express their thoughts.

9) avoid blame: rather than blaming or pointing fingers, focus on finding solutions together. if mistakes were made, approach them as learning experiences and opportunities for growth.

10) seek professional advice: in some situations, it might be helpful to involve a financial advisor or planner. their expertise can provide objective insights and help mediate discussions.

11) regular check-ins: make discussing money a regular part of your conversations, especially if you share financial responsibilities. regular check-ins can help identify issues early and adjust plans accordingly.

12) be prepared for change: financial situations can change over time due to various reasons. be prepared to adapt and modify plans as needed, and communicate these changes to your family and friends.

13) use "i" statements: when expressing concerns or opinions, use "i" statements to avoid sounding accusatory. for example, say "i feel concerned about our budget" rather than "you're spending too much."

14) celebrate achievements: celebrate financial milestones and achievements together. this reinforces positive behaviors and encourages everyone to stay focused on their goals.

remember, effective communication about money requires ongoing effort and a willingness to work together. by creating an environment of trust and understanding, you can navigate financial discussions with your family and friends successfully.

SEEKING PROFESSIONAL FINANCIAL ADVICE

seeking professional financial advice is a critical step toward achieving your financial goals and ensuring your long-term financial well-being. while it might be tempting to manage your finances on your own, a skilled financial advisor can provide you with expert guidance, tailored strategies, and a comprehensive understanding of complex financial matters.

here are some key points to consider when seeking professional financial advice:

1) expertise and knowledge: financial advisors possess a deep understanding of various financial concepts, including investment strategies, tax planning, retirement planning, estate planning, risk management, and more. their knowledge helps them analyze your unique financial situation and develop suitable recommendations.

2) personalized approach: a good financial advisor takes the time to understand your specific goals, risk tolerance, time horizon, and current financial situation. this enables them to create a personalized financial plan that aligns with your objectives.

3) objective perspective: emotional biases can often cloud our judgment when making financial decisions. a financial advisor provides an objective viewpoint and helps you make rational choices based on facts and analysis rather than emotions.

4) comprehensive financial planning: financial advisors help you create a holistic financial plan that considers all aspects of your financial life, from budgeting and saving to investing and retirement planning. this

comprehensive approach ensures that no critical elements are overlooked.

5) investment guidance: navigating the world of investments can be complex and overwhelming. a financial advisor can help you design an investment portfolio that matches your risk tolerance, financial goals, and time horizon. they monitor the portfolio's performance and make adjustments as needed.

6) risk management: financial advisors can assess your risk exposure and recommend strategies to mitigate potential risks. this could include insurance coverage, emergency funds, and diversification in investments.

7) tax efficiency: a financial advisor can help you optimize your tax strategy by identifying tax-saving opportunities, managing tax implications of investments, and suggesting tax-efficient investment vehicles.

8) retirement planning: planning for retirement involves careful consideration of factors such as savings, investment returns, social security, and more. a financial advisor can help you determine how much you need to save and invest to maintain your desired lifestyle in retirement.

9) estate planning: if you have significant assets, an estate plan is crucial for ensuring a smooth transfer of wealth to your heirs while minimizing taxes and legal complications. a financial advisor can work with estate planning attorneys to develop an effective strategy.

10) continuous monitoring and adjustments: financial markets and personal circumstances can change over time. a financial advisor regularly reviews your financial plan, makes necessary adjustments, and keeps you on track toward your goals.

11) credentials and regulation: when choosing a financial advisor, look for credentials such as certified financial planner (cfp), chartered financial analyst (cfa), or certified public accountant (cpa). additionally,

ensure that the advisor is registered with appropriate regulatory bodies to maintain ethical and professional standards.

12) fees and compensation: different advisors have various fee structures, including commission-based, fee-only, or a combination. it's important to understand how your advisor is compensated and to clarify any potential conflicts of interest.

in conclusion, seeking professional financial advice is a prudent step to take control of your financial future. a qualified financial advisor can offer valuable insights, create a tailored financial plan, and help you navigate the complexities of financial decision-making, ultimately increasing your chances of achieving your financial goals.

CHAPTER EIGHT

SUSTAINING POSITIVE CHANGE

sustaining positive change involves the continued maintenance and reinforcement of beneficial modifications in various aspects of life, whether they are personal, societal, or organizational. achieving positive change is a significant accomplishment, but ensuring its continuity over the long term can be just as challenging. here are some key factors and strategies to consider when aiming to sustain positive change:

1) clear goals and vision: having a clear understanding of the desired outcome is essential. whether it's improving one's health, promoting environmental sustainability, or enhancing workplace culture, a well-defined vision provides direction and motivation for the change effort.

2) gradual implementation: rushing change can lead to burnout and resistance. gradually introducing modifications allows individuals and systems to adapt and integrate the changes into their routines, increasing the likelihood of long-term success.

3) behavioral reinforcement: positive change often involves altering behaviors. employ strategies like positive reinforcement, rewards, and recognition to encourage the continuation of new habits and actions.

4) education and awareness: keep stakeholders informed about the benefits of the change and the progress made. by understanding the positive impact, individuals are more likely to remain engaged and committed to sustaining the change.

5) measurement and evaluation: regularly track and measure the progress of the change initiative. collect data on key performance indicators to assess the impact and identify areas that require adjustment.

6) adaptability: circumstances may change over time, and flexibility is crucial. be prepared to adapt strategies and approaches to fit evolving needs and challenges.

7) leadership and role modeling: strong leadership sets the tone for sustaining positive change. leaders should consistently demonstrate the desired behaviors and actively support the change effort to inspire others.

8) cultural integration: embed the change within the culture of the organization or community. when the change becomes part of the norm, it is more likely to be sustained.

9) community and peer support: establish a supportive environment where individuals can share their experiences, challenges, and successes. peer support and community involvement create a sense of accountability and camaraderie.

10) communication: maintain open and transparent communication channels. address concerns, answer questions, and provide updates regularly to keep stakeholders engaged and informed.

11) training and skill development: equip individuals with the necessary skills and knowledge to sustain the change. training programs can empower people to continue practicing new behaviors effectively.

12) celebrate milestones: celebrate achievements along the way. acknowledging progress reinforces the positive impact of the change effort and boosts morale.

13) long-term perspective: sustaining positive change requires a long-term perspective. acknowledge that setbacks may occur, but focus on learning from them and continuing the journey toward the desired outcome.

14) data-driven approach: use data and feedback to make informed decisions about adjustments and improvements. regular analysis of data can help identify trends and areas that need further attention.

15) institutionalization: if possible, integrate the change into policies, procedures, and structures to ensure its longevity even as personnel or leadership changes.

ultimately, sustaining positive change is a dynamic process that requires ongoing effort, dedication, and a holistic approach. by addressing various factors and adopting appropriate strategies, individuals and organizations can increase the likelihood of maintaining the positive changes they have worked hard to achieve.

DEALING WITH SETBACKS AND STAYING MOTIVATED

dealing with setbacks and staying motivated are essential skills for navigating the ups and downs of life. setbacks are inevitable, but how you respond to them can greatly impact your overall success and well-being. here's an extensive overview of strategies to effectively handle setbacks and maintain motivation:

1. embrace resilience:

resilience is the ability to bounce back from adversity. cultivate this trait by acknowledging your feelings, but also reframing challenges as opportunities for growth. understand that setbacks are a natural part of any journey and can provide valuable lessons.

2. maintain perspective:
when setbacks occur, it's easy to lose sight of the bigger picture. remind yourself of your long-term goals and how this setback fits into the grand scheme of things. often, setbacks are just temporary roadblocks on your path to success.

3. learn from failure:
view setbacks as learning experiences. analyze what went wrong and identify lessons that can be applied to future endeavors. failure is a stepping stone to success; many successful individuals have faced multiple failures before achieving their goals.

4. set realistic expectations:
unrealistic expectations can lead to disappointment and demotivation. set achievable goals that challenge you without overwhelming your capabilities. this way, even if setbacks occur, they won't derail your entire motivation.

5. break down goals:
large goals can feel overwhelming, making setbacks seem insurmountable. break down your goals into smaller, manageable tasks. this allows you to focus on incremental progress and celebrate small victories along the way.

6. practice self-compassion:
be kind to yourself during setbacks. avoid self-blame and negative self-talk. treat yourself with the same kindness and understanding you would offer to a friend facing a similar situation.

7. seek support:
don't be afraid to reach out for support from friends, family, mentors, or professionals. sharing your feelings and experiences can help alleviate stress and provide fresh perspectives on how to overcome setbacks.

8. adapt and pivot:
setbacks often require adapting to new circumstances. be open to
adjusting your approach or trying new strategies. flexibility and
adaptability are key traits in overcoming obstacles.

9. visualization and affirmations:
visualizing success and using positive affirmations can help maintain
motivation during challenging times. envisioning your desired outcome
can keep you focused on the end goal, even when setbacks arise.

10. stay consistent:
consistency is crucial for maintaining motivation. establish routines that
keep you engaged with your goals, even when setbacks occur.
consistency helps you stay connected to your aspirations and prevents
demotivation.

11. celebrate progress:
acknowledge and celebrate your achievements, no matter how small.
recognizing your progress, even in the face of setbacks, reinforces a
positive mindset and boosts motivation.

12. practice mindfulness:
mindfulness techniques, such as meditation and deep breathing, can
help manage stress and anxiety caused by setbacks. being present in the
moment can reduce negative thoughts and help you refocus on your
goals.

13. find inspiration:
seek inspiration from various sources, such as books, podcasts, or role
models. learning about others' journeys and how they overcame setbacks
can provide a fresh perspective on your own challenges.

14. setbacks as feedback:
view setbacks as feedback on your approach rather than personal
failures. this shift in mindset allows you to identify areas for
improvement and adjust your strategies accordingly.

15. focus on what you can control:
while you can't control every aspect of a situation, you can control your response and actions. direct your energy toward things you can influence, and let go of factors beyond your control.

in summary, setbacks are a natural part of life, and staying motivated through challenges requires a combination of resilience, perspective, and adaptive strategies. by cultivating these skills and maintaining a positive outlook, you can navigate setbacks with grace and continue progressing toward your goals.

CELEBRATING MILESTONES AND ACHIEVEMENT

celebrating milestones and achievements holds a significant place in human culture and psychology. these events mark important moments of progress, growth, and success, providing individuals and communities with a sense of accomplishment and motivation. whether it's a personal achievement like graduating from school, a professional milestone such as completing a project, or a collective accomplishment like reaching a company's annual goal, celebrating these moments has various positive impacts.

1) recognition and validation: celebrations acknowledge the efforts and hard work that have gone into reaching a goal. they provide individuals with validation for their dedication, perseverance, and commitment. this recognition fosters a sense of pride and boosts self-esteem, encouraging individuals to continue striving for excellence.

2) motivation and inspiration: celebrating milestones and achievements serves as a source of motivation and inspiration for both the person accomplishing the feat and those around them. sharing success stories and acknowledging progress can motivate others to set their own goals and work towards them with determination.

3) positive reinforcement: positive reinforcement plays a vital role in behavior psychology. celebrating achievements reinforces the behavior and actions that led to success, making it more likely for individuals to

repeat those actions in the future. this is especially important in educational and professional settings.

4) building a positive culture: in organizations, celebrating achievements contributes to creating a positive and collaborative work culture. it fosters a sense of camaraderie and team spirit, encouraging employees to support one another's success and collaborate effectively.

5) marking milestones of growth: personal and professional growth is often marked by milestones and achievements. celebrating these moments allows individuals to reflect on their journey, from where they started to where they are now. this reflection can be a source of personal satisfaction and motivation to continue evolving.

6) strengthening relationships: celebrations bring people together, whether it's a family gathering for a graduation or a team celebrating a project's successful completion. these events provide opportunities for bonding, networking, and forming deeper connections with others who share in the joy of the achievement.

7) creating lasting memories: special occasions like milestone celebrations create cherished memories that individuals can look back on with fondness. these memories often serve as reminders of the progress made and the hurdles overcome, serving as a source of inspiration during challenging times.

8) promoting goal setting: celebrating achievements encourages individuals to set new goals and pursue further growth. by reflecting on what they've accomplished, individuals can identify areas for improvement and set higher aspirations.

9) boosting overall well-being: celebrations trigger the release of dopamine, a neurotransmitter associated with pleasure and reward. this leads to an overall positive impact on mental and emotional well-being, contributing to reduced stress and enhanced happiness.

10) cultural and social significance: celebrating milestones is deeply ingrained in human culture and tradition. these celebrations often have

cultural, religious, or social significance, enriching the tapestry of human experience and connecting people across time and geography.

in conclusion, celebrating milestones and achievements is more than just a moment of revelry. it's a way to acknowledge hard work, inspire others, reinforce positive behaviors, and build a sense of community. by recognizing and commemorating these significant moments, individuals and groups can derive a multitude of psychological, social, and emotional benefits that contribute to their personal and collective growth.

CHAPTER NINE

CASE STUDIES: REAL-LIFE TRANSFORMATIONS

real-life case studies are powerful examples of how organizations or individuals have undergone significant transformations to overcome challenges, achieve goals, or adapt to changing circumstances. these case studies provide valuable insights into the strategies, tactics, and approaches employed to drive successful change. here are a few notable examples of real-life transformations:

1) netflix's evolution: netflix began as a dvd rental-by-mail service but underwent a massive transformation into a streaming media powerhouse. by recognizing the shift in consumer behavior towards digital content consumption, netflix shifted its focus towards online streaming. this strategic transformation not only changed the way people watch tv shows and movies but also disrupted the traditional entertainment industry.

2) apple's resurgence: in the late 1990s, apple was struggling financially and facing fierce competition. steve jobs returned to the company and orchestrated a remarkable transformation. apple shifted its focus from a niche computer manufacturer to a consumer electronics and software giant. the introduction of the ipod, followed by the iphone and ipad,

catapulted apple to become one of the most valuable companies in the world.

3) starbucks' global expansion: starbucks began as a single coffee shop in seattle. through careful branding, customer experience, and innovative store concepts, it successfully expanded into a global coffeehouse chain. starbucks' transformation wasn't just about selling coffee; it was about selling an experience, a "third place" between work and home.

4) lego's turnaround: in the early 2000s, lego was on the brink of bankruptcy due to financial mismanagement and competition from digital entertainment. by returning to its core values of creative play and interlocking bricks, lego transformed itself into a toy and media company with a strong focus on imagination and innovation.

5) domino's pizza reinvention: domino's faced criticism for the quality of its pizzas. in response, the company launched an ambitious transformation campaign, admitting its shortcomings and pledging to improve. through innovative recipes, transparency, and a renewed commitment to customer feedback, domino's turned its negative reputation around and experienced a significant increase in sales.

6) amazon's growth strategy: amazon started as an online bookstore but quickly transformed into a global e-commerce giant. over time, it expanded its offerings to include cloud computing services (amazon web services), digital streaming (amazon prime video), smart devices (amazon echo), and more. amazon's focus on customer-centricity and relentless innovation drove its transformation and market dominance.

7) tesla's electric revolution: tesla disrupted the automotive industry by transforming electric cars from a niche concept to a desirable and innovative product. through cutting-edge technology, sleek designs, and a commitment to sustainable transportation, tesla has spurred other automakers to invest heavily in electric vehicle development.

8) mcdonald's healthier menu: responding to changing consumer preferences, mcdonald's underwent a transformation by introducing

healthier menu options, reducing trans fats, and offering more transparency about nutritional information. this move aimed to address concerns about fast food's impact on health and nutrition.

real-life case studies like these offer valuable lessons for businesses and individuals looking to navigate change and achieve growth. they showcase the importance of adaptability, innovation, customer-centricity, and strategic planning in the face of challenges and evolving market landscapes. by analyzing these transformations, stakeholders can gain insights into the strategies and approaches that drive successful change initiatives.

STORIES OF INDIVIDUALS WHO OVERCAME POOR MONEY HABITS

certainly! stories of individuals who have overcome poor money habits can be incredibly inspiring and serve as examples for others looking to improve their financial situations. here are a few noteworthy examples:

1) dave ramsey: dave ramsey is a well-known personal finance expert who went from bankruptcy to financial success. he accumulated significant debt in his early adult life but managed to turn his life around by adopting a strict budget, cutting unnecessary expenses, and using the "snowball method" to pay off his debts. he has since become a renowned author, radio host, and speaker, helping millions of people achieve financial independence.

2) suze orman: suze orman grew up with very little financial education and made several poor money decisions in her early years. however, she managed to turn her life around by learning about personal finance and investing. she worked as a waitress and saved aggressively to start her own business. today, she is a best-selling author and a respected financial advisor, helping others take control of their finances.

3) trent hamm: trent hamm is the founder of "the simple dollar," a popular personal finance blog. he struggled with excessive spending, credit card debt, and poor financial decisions. through research and

determination, he learned how to live frugally, pay off his debts, and manage his finances wisely. he now shares his experiences and insights on his blog, helping others make positive changes in their financial lives.

4) elizabeth warren: before becoming a u.s. senator and a prominent figure in american politics, elizabeth warren faced personal financial challenges. as a young mother, she dealt with job loss and financial instability. she went on to pursue education and eventually became a law professor. her experiences with financial difficulties led her to research and advocate for better consumer protection laws and financial regulation.

5) chris hogan: chris hogan, a former football player and now a financial coach, struggled with debt and poor money habits early in his career. he managed to eliminate his debt and establish a strong financial foundation by following a disciplined plan, living below his means, and making wise investment choices. he now helps individuals achieve their financial goals through coaching, speaking engagements, and his books.

these stories emphasize the importance of determination, education, and making intentional choices when it comes to managing money. they demonstrate that with the right mindset and strategies, anyone can overcome poor money habits and achieve financial success.

CONCLUSION

EMBRACING A FUTURE OF FINANCIAL WELL-BEING

embracing a future of financial well-being is a pivotal aspect of leading a fulfilling and balanced life. it involves a proactive and mindful approach to managing one's finances, ensuring stability, freedom, and the ability to pursue one's goals and dreams. this concept encompasses a variety of principles and practices that contribute to a strong financial foundation.

1. financial literacy: the first step towards achieving financial well-being is acquiring knowledge about financial concepts, such as budgeting,

saving, investing, and debt management. being financially literate empowers individuals to make informed decisions and avoid pitfalls that can lead to financial stress.

2. goal setting: setting clear financial goals is crucial. whether it's buying a home, funding education, starting a business, or retiring comfortably, having well-defined objectives provides direction and motivation for managing money effectively.

3. budgeting: creating and adhering to a budget is fundamental. it helps track income and expenses, identify areas for improvement, and ensure that money is allocated appropriately to meet various needs and desires.

4. emergency fund: establishing an emergency fund acts as a safety net during unexpected financial setbacks, such as medical expenses, job loss, or major repairs. a common recommendation is to save three to six months' worth of living expenses.

5. debt management: responsible management of debt involves minimizing high-interest debt and paying it off systematically. this can relieve financial stress and free up resources for other important goals.

6. saving and investing: regular saving and investing enable the growth of wealth over time. diversifying investments, understanding risk tolerance, and aligning investment strategies with long-term goals are key components of this aspect.

7. retirement planning: planning for retirement ensures a comfortable and secure future. contributing to retirement accounts, such as 401(k)s or iras, can help build a nest egg that provides financial freedom during one's golden years.

8. mindful spending: being mindful of spending habits encourages responsible consumption. prioritizing needs over wants and making intentional spending choices can prevent unnecessary financial strain.

9. continuous learning: the financial landscape is constantly evolving. staying updated on market trends, investment options, and new financial tools can help individuals make well-informed decisions.

10. seek professional advice: consulting with financial advisors or experts can provide personalized guidance tailored to individual circumstances. they can help create customized financial plans and strategies to achieve specific goals.

11. psychological well-being: financial well-being is not solely about numbers; it also involves psychological and emotional factors. reducing financial stress and anxiety contributes to overall well-being.

12. generosity and giving: embracing financial well-being can also include contributing to causes and helping others in need. acts of generosity and charitable giving can provide a sense of purpose and fulfillment.

13. adaptability: life is full of unexpected changes. embracing financial well-being involves being adaptable and having contingency plans to navigate through challenges and seize opportunities.

in conclusion, embracing a future of financial well-being requires a holistic approach that combines knowledge, discipline, and adaptability. it's about creating a solid financial foundation that supports personal and professional aspirations, while also contributing to overall happiness and contentment. by adopting these principles and practices, individuals can work towards a more secure and fulfilling financial future.